JOHN CARNEY'S
TASTE OF
RESTAURANT
TUESDAY

JOHN CARNEY'S TASTE OF RESTAURANT TUESDAY

Copyright © 2006 Carney's Kids Foundation
Cover illustration by Dan Martin

Published by Virginia Publishing Company for Carney's Kids Foundation

ISBN: 1-891442-41-4

Library of Congress Control Number: 2006931828

Please note: Recipes in this book have been written and submitted by many different restaurants over the years. While the publisher has edited them and has had professional chefs review the recipes, the publisher and Carney's Kids Foundation can not be held responsible for restaurant-submitted recipes which may contain errors or inconsistencies in style. Further, the publisher and Carney's Kids Foundation can not guarantee that recipes submitted by restaurants will turn out exactly as described.

Editors: Fran Levy, Kimberly Marlowe
Proofreading: MJ McNeece, Tim Woodcock
Book Design: James Macanufo

Virginia Publishing Company
PO Box 4538
St. Louis, MO 63108
www.STL-Books.com
Printed in China

TABLE OF CONTENTS

FOREWORD

You hold in your hands a treasure trove.

Pretty much every day at the "Let's Eat" section of the *Post-Dispatch*, we get one or two letters, calls or e-mails asking for this or that St. Louis restaurant recipe – sometimes from a place where someone has just dined, sometimes from some long-closed restaurant that nonetheless lives on as a very fond memory.

Well, here are more than 200 answers, all in one place. Not only that, but you'll also find some of the most frequently requested recipes from John's late father, the legendary KMOX personality Jack Carney.

I've been lucky enough to trade tidbits of restaurant news and gossip – along with the frequent verbal sparring, all in fun (I think) – with John Carney for some four years now. My KMOX minor celebrity is all John's doing: Although we'd met in passing a few times, we didn't really know each other very well when he called me out of the blue one day and asked me to contribute to the Restaurant Tuesday version of his show.

We talk about the stuff he hears and the stuff I hear. The conversations opened up a great pipeline for me, because every Wednesday morning, like clockwork, I get calls and e-mails with more comments and tips on what's going on in the local restaurant community.

More important, though – and if you ever tell him I said this, I'll deny it – as we got to know each other, I found out that John is an incredibly thoughtful and caring guy. His occasionally acerbic wit masks an honest and deeply held commitment to helping children in need, as realized through his Carney's Kids Foundation. Your purchase of this book will help John to continue his great charitable work.

Thanks for buying it, and I hope you enjoy the recipes as much as I have!

Joe Bonwich
Food writer and restaurant critic
St. Louis Post-Dispatch
July 2006

INTRODUCTION

One can never determine, ahead of time, how somebody's love of food will develop.

I was lucky as a child and had an opportunity to dine in several parts of the world by the time I was 5. Most memorable was a wild hedgehog cooked on a spit, in a lightning storm, in East Africa. Back stateside, my earliest memories are of tugging on the apron strings of my nanny, Maria, who was from South America. She would regularly make piallas, posole and other dishes native to her homeland. When we didn't eat at home, it was always out to an exotic restaurant, where we either sat on the floor or had to take our shoes off. Later, in my adolescence, we had a live-in cook from Pakistan. Siraj would go through curry like we use butter. The smell of the piping hot flatbreads, roasted lambs and coucous is still very fresh in my mind. The funny thing about him was, he couldn't make an omelet or a sandwich to save his life. But I was content to chow down on some falafel or Tabuleah instead. All of this instilled in me a great curiosity about food that remains to this very day.

I would love to say that it was dear old mom's cooking that turned me, but sadly, I can't even picture her near the kitchen. Dad, on the other hand, wouldn't eat anything unless it had at least two unpronounceable ingredients. Like me, he enjoyed fiery foods, although, to everyone around him, it was obvious that he was experiencing a certain amount of suffering. To the best of my recollection, he was handy in the kitchen too. To this day, I still get listeners asking for his chili, chocolate chip cookie, and oyster stuffing recipes. In his honor, I have actually included them in this book.

My abilities in the kitchen have come over time. Even with all of the great foods I was treated to as a child, I never paid much attention to their preparation. This became painfully apparent as I set out on my own at the age of 15. Outside of the staple single-guy dishes of Ramen noodles, mac and cheese and canned soups, I was clueless as to how to prepare as much as a sandwich. Early disasters included Cornish game hens stuffed with canned tamales, and a 12-egg omelet. It took a dozen eggs because I thought you only used the yolks. It seemed like an obvious conclusion, as the dish was yellow, right?

It was through trial and error that I began to put things on plates that people could at least recognize. I was also fortunate enough as a teenager to get some jobs behind some stoves, most memorably a short order cook on the Admiral riverboat. I was charged with making fried chicken for 1200 people in a deep fryer that resembled a baby pool in an outdoor kitchen in August. This was all before child labor laws were put into effect. Catering gigs with Italian restaurants and schlepping home-style dinners at a mom-and-pop joint in Wright City also contributed to my culinary awakening.

In adulthood, I have been able to nurture my love of food, surrounding myself with great chefs and adventures of my own. My 40th birthday found me in Tuscany for a few weeks, making pasta dishes with Italian master Guiliano Bugialli.

Here's where my theory about one's passion for food comes in. I have tried to give my children the same exposure to worldly cuisines that I had. My oldest was eating sopapillas in Cancun when she was 9 months old. Both of my girls dined on Peking duck in a rather seedy joint in Beijing. Yet, despite my best efforts, the dish that garners the most reaction is a McDonalds Happy Meal. Well, maybe after they get their hands on a stale fruit roll up, their hearts will turn.

On to this project. I started having restaurants on the radio back in 1992 when I worked at WEW. This always led to battles with management, as it was their belief that this was just a quick way for me to garner a free meal. They were partially right. I also felt it was important for these mom and pop places to get some exposure. Anyone who would willfully invest their time and money into an industry that has a 90% failure rate deserves my support. I have had a few hard and fast rules with the feature over the years: Avoid chains (mostly because they could afford to advertise) and no repeats. I have had several folks who have made a few appearances on the program, but that has been because they have opened a new place or surfaced at someone else's joint.

Each restaurant featured on Restaurant Tuesday is asked to bring in a few things. First off: Food for 10. Usually there are just 4 or 5 of us there at the time, but you can't be too careful. Also, 4 gift certificates, which we give away or save for a future time (for the record, I have never used one of them myself). And they also need to provide a recipe from one of their popular dishes. This was because it has always been my intention to put out a cookbook for charity. Now that we have formed Carney's Kids, what a perfect time!

When I sat down to count them, the number cleared 400. As this was not going to be a Nancy Drew-type series, I had to pare things down a bit. I found I had several recipes for the same thing, so I picked the ones that seemed less complicated, bumping things like the chicken salad recipe that called for sun-poached, free-range Amish chickens!! Sadly, that 90% failure rate drove itself home as I separated the recipes from eateries that were no longer with us. I'd like to think that their appearance on my show had little to do with that.

Here comes the disclaimer! I would love to tell you that I tried each and everyone of these recipes, but it was just not possible. The ones that I have made have become staples in my kitchen. Some others are things you would find on a menu's heart-healthy menu, which, simply put, means I probably didn't even know they made it. What I can tell you is that these are dishes of which the restaurants thought highly enough to offer them to me. I now, most humbly, offer them up to you. Bon appetit.

- John

APPETIZERS

1860'S HARD SHELL CAFÉ AND BAR

1860 S. 9th 314-231-1860

OLD-FASHIONED CREOLE CORN BREAD

Ingredients
2 cups yellow corn meal
1 cup all purpose flour
1/2 cup tomato, diced
1/2 cup jalapeno peppers, diced
3 tsp. baking powder
1/2 cup sugar
2 eggs
1-1/2 tsp. salt
1/2 cup bacon drippings
milk

PREPARATION

In a large bowl, mix all ingredients together, except milk. Stir until well blended. Add enough milk to make mixture pour easily. Spoon into greased muffin tins.
Bake in 400-degree oven 20-30 minutes.

SERVES 8

ALMONDS

8127 Maryland Ave. 314-725-1019

TASSO STREUDEL

Ingredients
1 box phyllo dough
1/2 cup green bell peppers, chopped
1/2 cup onions, chopped
1 lb. Monterey jack cheese, grated
1 cup tasso, chopped
1/2 cup melted butter

Sauté the onions and peppers until tender, and allow to cool. Place the phyllo dough on a flat surface (cutting board) and cut into four equal parts. Using a pastry brush, butter the top half of the phyllo dough.

Place equal parts cheese and tasso (1/2 tsp. each) on the bottom of each row and add 1/2 tsp. of peppers and onions on top. Fold the top three sheets of dough like a paper football (corner to corner). Seal the last fold with the buttered end. Repeat until all sheets and filling are used up. Cook at 400 degrees for 15-20 minutes or until brown. Makes great party snacks.

CAFÉ BALABAN

405 N. Euclid Ave. 314-361-8085

CORN PANCAKE WITH SMOKED TROUT AND HORSERADISH SAUCE

Ingredients for Smoked Trout and Horseradish Topping
3/4 cup smoked trout, broken into bite-sized pieces
1/2 cup mayonnaise
2 oz. prepared horseradish, drained

Ingredients for Corn Pancake

1 cup corn, blanched and removed from the ears
1/2 cup milk
3 large eggs
1/2 cup (by volume) semolina
1 cup corn, blanched and removed from the ears
1/2 cup red onion, finely diced
1/4 cup chives or scallions, chopped
2 tsp. olive oil
1/2 tsp. salt
1 tsp. black pepper
1 tsp. baking powder
1 oz. chives, chopped, for garnish

PREPARATION

Combine smoked trout, mayonnaise, and horseradish in a bowl and fold together. Set aside.

Combine 1 cup corn and 1/2 cup milk in a blender. Puree and strain through a fine strainer. Reserve
   liquid.

Mix eggs in a medium bowl until homogenous. Add reserved pureed corn. Mix in semolina, red onion,
   chives, 1 tsp. olive oil, salt, pepper, corn, and baking powder.
In a non-stick skillet over low heat add 1 tsp. of olive oil. When oil becomes slightly hot, add 2 oz. corn
   pancake batter for each pancake. Cook pancakes until bubbles form. Flip and brown on other side.
   Remove from heat and place on serving dishes.

Divide trout mixture evenly on top of the four pancakes. Sprinkle with fresh chives.

SERVES 4

BEVO MILL

4749 Gravois Ave. 314-481-2626 www.bevomill.com

BEVO MILL'S FAMOUS CHEDDAR CHEESE & CHIVE BISCUITS

Ingredients
2 lbs. flour
2 tsp. salt
4-1/2 Tbs. baking powder
2/3 cup sugar
1/4 cup dried chives
3/4 cup cheddar, grated
1/2 cup oil
2/3 cup melted margarine
2-3/4 cups milk

PREPARATION

Mix all dry ingredients together thoroughly. Add butter and oil, stirring until oils are mixed in. Add milk and knead just until mix pulls away from side of bowl. (Do not over mix.) Drop onto baking pan from a large spoon. Each biscuit should weigh about 2 oz. Cook in 400-degree oven about 20 minutes or until done.

YIELDS 2-1/2 DOZEN 2-OZ. BISCUITS

MUSSELS STEAMED WITH SAFFRON CURRY CREAM

Ingredients

2/3 lb. Prince Edward Island mussels per person, or any other fresh mussels, rinsed in cold water and beards removed
1 Tbs. butter
1 small yellow onion, diced small
2 cloves garlic, peeled and minced
1 Braeburn apple, diced small
1-1/2 Tbs. fresh ginger, peeled, grated and pulp discarded
1/4 cup brandy
2 cups white wine
2/3 cup apple juice, no sugar added
1 pinch saffron thread
1/3 Tbs. mild curry powder
1/3 Tbs. lemon zest
1/3 Tbs. dried thyme
1 small bay leaf
1 small dried chili pepper, santaka or pasilla
2 tsp. fresh lemon juice
1 cup heavy cream

PREPARATION

Sweat onions, garlic, ginger and apples in butter in a covered saucepan over low heat until soft. Increase heat and deglaze with brandy (always use caution when deglazing with liquor; beware of flames). After flame dies out, add white wine, apple juice, saffron thread, curry powder, lemon zest, thyme, bay leaf, chili pepper, and lemon juice and bring to boil. Reduce to simmer and cook until reduced by half. Add heavy cream and simmer another five minutes. Add salt and pepper to taste. (The sauce, up to this point, can be made up to one day in advance.)

Heat mussels in sauce until they open and the sauce boils. Discard any mussels that do not open. Serve immediately with crusty bread for dipping.

SAUCE YIELD: ONE QUART; EIGHT 4-OZ. SERVINGS
DOUBLE PORTIONS FOR ENTREES

CAFÉ MANHATTAN

511 S. Hanley Rd. 314-863-4703

MANHATTAN BRUSCHETTA

Ingredients
1 cup artichoke hearts, crushed
1 cup grated Parmesan cheese
1/4 cup grated cheddar
3/4 cup mayonnaise
1 tsp. crushed garlic

PREPARATION

Mix all ingredients thoroughly. Spread to 1/4-inch thickness on sliced sourdough. Broil until golden brown. Serve immediately.

CHEVY'S FRESH MEX

1600 Heritage Landing, Suite 200 636-926-0505

SWEET CORN TOMALITO

Ingredients
1/2 lb. soft margarine
1 cup masa for tamales (can be purchased at most Mexican shops)
1-1/4 cups sugar
1-1/2 cups water
1-1/2 cups corn meal
1 Tbs. baking powder
1/2 Tbs. salt
1/2 cup milk
2-1/2 lbs. corn kernels, thawed

PREPARATION

Whip the soft margarine, masa, and sugar together until light and fluffy (approximately two minutes). Blend half of the corn kernels with water until smooth. Combine this mixture along with the rest of the ingredients. Mix well.

Pour corn mixture in a shallow pan, and tightly cover with plastic wrap. Steam for 60 - 75 minutes until mixture is smooth and moist. Serve in a covered dish to keep moist texture.

** Shelf life for this dish is two days.

YIELDS 82 (2-OZ.) PORTIONS

THE CROSSING

7823 Forsyth Blvd. 314-721-7375

BLUE CHEESE SOUFFLÉ

Ingredients
1 cup blue cheese, grated
1 cup cheddar, grated
1 cup onion, diced
1 egg
1/4 cup milk
1 cup mayonnaise
salt and pepper

Mix all ingredients together and spoon into a ramekin. Place in a water bath and bake at 300 degrees for 30-40 minutes until brown. Serve hot.

THE DELMAR

6235 Delmar 314-725-6565

CRAWFISH CAKES

Ingredients
2 lbs. crawfish tails, thawed and well drained
1 small red pepper, minced
1 small red onion, minced
1 stalk celery, minced
2 eggs
3/4 cup mayonnaise
1/8 cup honey
1/2 cup grain mustard
1 Tbs. chili powder
1/2 Tbs. cumin
generous pinch salt
generous pinch pepper
1/2 Tbs. Old Bay spice
2-1/2 cups breadcrumbs
butter

Mix by hand. Portion into patties. Pan-fry with butter on medium heat until golden brown.

Cajun Mayo Ingredients
3/4 cup salad oil
1 egg yolk
1/2 Tbs. Dijon mustard
3/4 tsp. chili powder
3/4 tsp. cumin
1/4 tsp. salt
generous pinch white pepper
1/2 tsp. lemon juice
1 Tbs. water

Place yolks and mustard into food processor and mix well. Add the spices and lemon juice and mix well. Slowly add half of the oil while the processor is running, then add the water and the rest of the oil. Garnish with thinly sliced pieces of grilled andouille sausage.

7

DIABLO CAFÉ

DIABLO CAFÉ CRAB CAKES

Ingredients
8 oz. crabmeat
1 Tbs. celery, diced
1 Tbs. yellow onion, diced
1/2 cup plain breadcrumbs
1/2 tsp. fresh garlic, chopped
pinch of salt and pepper
1/4 cup mayonnaise
1 whole egg
1 tsp. lemon juice
pinch cayenne pepper
1 tsp. olive oil

Ingredients for Sauce:
1 tsp. strained jalapeno pepper
salt and pepper
1 cup sour cream
1 tsp. strained roasted bell pepper
1 cup sour cream

PREPARATION

Sauté celery, onion and garlic in olive oil, remove from heat and let cool. Blend all ingredients together. For the sauce, puree strained jalapeño pepper, a pinch of salt and pepper with 1/2 cup of sour cream. Set aside. Purée strained roasted bell peppers with a pinch of salt and pepper with 1/2 cup of sour cream. Set aside. Drizzle and stripe the crab cakes with the 2 sauces to finish the presentation of the dish with added color and flavor. Serve and enjoy!

FLEMING'S PRIME STEAKHOUSE & WINE BAR

1855 S. Lindbergh Blvd. 314-567-7610

PACIFIC RIM BEEF ROLLS

Ingredients
4 lbs. meat trimmings
4 Tbs. sesame oil
4 tsp. black pepper
12 oz. yellow onion
1 lb. portobello mushrooms
2 Tbs. garlic, minced
1 lb. red cabbage
2 bunches green onions
1/4 cup soy sauce
1/2 cup rice wine vinegar
2 Tbs. corn starch
2 Tbs. water

SERVICE PREPARATION

Cutting board, chef's knife, measuring spoon, scale, fryer, sheet pan, chef's tongs, food processor, sauté pan, serving platter.

PREPARATION

Trim any tough fat from meat trimmings and cut meat into very thin bite-sized slices. Put 2 Tbs. sesame oil in large saucepot, set on high heat. When hot, add meat and season with black pepper. Cook meat for 3-4 minutes. Drain cooked meat in colander and discard fat. Mince onion and remove stem and gills from portobello. Cut portobello into thin strips 1/8 inch wide by 2 inch long. Return pot to range, set on medium high heat and add 2 Tbs. oil. Add onions and portobello mushrooms; cook for 3-4 minutes. Add minced garlic and cook for 2 minutes. Shred red cabbage and add to pot. Cook for 2-3 minutes. Add soy and rice wine vinegar to pot and bring to a light boil. Combine cornstarch and water together and mix well. Add to pot and mix well. Cut ends off green onions and then cut entire onion into 1/4 inch wide.

THE GRILL; THE RITZ-CARLTON, ST. LOUIS

100 Carondelet Plaza 314-863-6300

RITZ-CARLTON CRAB CAKES

Ingredients
2 lbs. jumbo crabmeat or flaked crabmeat
1 green pepper, skin, seeds and membrane removed, diced
1 red pepper, skin, seeds and membrane removed, diced
3 Tbs. clarified butter
3 Tbs. flour
1 cup white wine
2 Tbs. prepared mustard
ground pepper and salt to taste

PREPARATION

Sauté green and red pepper until heated through but still firm in the clarified butter. Add the flour and white wine. Cook ingredients until thick. Remove from the heat. Add the prepared mustard, pepper and salt. Add crabmeat. Shape into cakes. Sauté in the butter until brown. Serve the cakes with Lemon Caper Beurre Blanc Sauce (see recipe).

Lemon Caper Beurre Blanc Sauce
Ingredients
olive oil
1 small finely chopped shallot
1 cup dry white wine
2 tsp. vinegar
1/2 cup heavy cream
1/2 lb. unsalted butter, softened
1/2 Tbs. lemon juice
1 Tbs. chopped capers

Sauté the shallot in oil until it is glossy. Add wine and vinegar. Simmer and reduce to half its original volume. Reduce heat and add the heavy cream. Heat until slowly simmering. Whisk in the softened butter a little at a time. Beat constantly with a sauce whisk until the sauce is creamy and whitened. Do not boil. Stir in the lemon juice and capers. Serve immediately.

HARD ROCK CAFÉ

450 St. Louis Union Station 314-621-7625 www.hardrock.com

HICKORY SMOKED CHICKEN & SPINACH DIP

Ingredients

8 oz. butter
1/2 cup pure olive oil
2-1/2 cups yellow onion, finely chopped
1/3 cup garlic, chopped
1 cup flour

1 quart chicken consommé
1 quart heavy cream
1 Tbs. + 1 tsp. Liquid Smoke

1/4 cup fresh lemon juice
3 Tbs. chicken base
1 Tbs. + 1 tsp. Tabasco sauce
1 Tbs. granulated sugar
1 Tbs. ground white pepper
2 cups grated Romano cheese
1-1/2 cups sour cream

3 lbs. frozen chopped spinach, thawed
2 lbs. oven poached chicken, 1/4 inch diced

PREPARATION

Melt butter with olive oil in a large pan or skillet. Do not allow the butter to brown. Add onions and garlic and cook until onions are soft (approximately 5 minutes). Create a roux by stirring in the flour until it is well incorporated by the butter/oil mixture and cook 3 minutes, stirring constantly. (It is important to stir constantly to prevent the flour from scorching the pan.)

Add a little (2 cups) of the consommé to temper the roux and stir thoroughly. Then add the remainder of the consommé. Bring to a boil and add the heavy cream and Liquid Smoke.
Bring back to a boil, then reduce heat and simmer for 3-5 minutes to ensure proper thickening of the filling. Once thickened, remove from the heat. Add lemon juice, chicken base, Tabasco sauce, sugar, white pepper, Romano cheese and sour cream. Stir well to evenly incorporate.

Once the spinach dip base has cooled to room temperature, fold in the spinach and incorporate well, using a large spoon or paddle. Fold in the diced chicken. Top with grated Monterey jack cheese, warm up mixture and serve, or refrigerate for later.

PORTOBELLO NAPOLEON

Ingredients
8 slices grilled eggplant, sliced 1/4-inch thick, 4 x 4 inch diameter
8 slices of roma tomatoes, cut lengthwise 1/4-inch thick
4 oz. fresh spinach, blanched
4 slices red onion, 1/4-inch thick
4 oz. fresh red pepper, 1/4-inch thick
6 oz. mozzarella cheese, shredded
4 medium portabello mushrooms
6 cloves garlic, chopped
10 leaves fresh basil
4 sprigs fresh rosemary
4 oz. olive oil

PREPARATION

Toss all ingredients in olive oil, chopped garlic and chopped basil. Season with salt and pepper. Char-grill the eggplant, peppers, onions and mushrooms. Remove from fire.

Layer all ingredients using a stack method: eggplant, tomato, spinach, mozzarella, eggplant and peppers. Top with portobello mushroom. Push rosemary sprig down the middle to use as skewer. Season with salt and pepper and place in oven to reheat at 350 degrees for approximately 5 minutes, and serve.

IRON BARLEY

5510 Virginia Ave. 314-351-4500

BARLEY WITH GRILLED VEGETABLES

Ingredients
1 medium eggplant, roughly chopped
1 zucchini, roughly chopped
1 yellow squash, roughly chopped
1 large or 2 small red onions
3/4 cup extra virgin olive oil
2-1/2 cups (about 1 lb.) pearled barley
10 cups pork stock or beef stock
salt and freshly ground pepper
2 cups processed tomato product (puree, ragout, etc.)
6 plum tomatoes, quartered

*Cast iron utensils are recommended, but not required.

PREPARATION

In a skillet or on a grill, cook eggplant, zucchini, squash and onion until onions are browned and vegetables are softened slightly, about 3 to 5 minutes. Remove from heat. Set a large pot over high heat. When pot is hot, add oil, heat just until oil shimmers and begins to smoke (watch carefully or oil will burst into flames). Add barley, cook, stirring constantly, until barley browns and then turns a reddish black, about 6 to 10 minutes. (Do not let burn.) Turn heat to low, pour in stock, return heat to high and bring to a boil, then reduce to a simmer. Cover and let simmer for 30 minutes, stirring occasionally. Add salt and pepper to taste. Increase heat to medium high, add tomato product. Cook until moderately thickened, about 10 minutes, stirring constantly. Add the grilled vegetables and quartered tomatoes, and bring to a boil. Let cool slightly. If desired, add salt and pepper.

SERVES 8 TO 12

JACK CARNEY'S OUT-OF-THIS-WORLD OUTHOUSE PICKLES

Ingredients
3-1/2 lbs. small pickling (Kirby) cucumbers, peels intact
1 cup hydrated lime
1 gallon water
1 qt. cider vinegar (5% acid content)
4 cups sugar
1/2 tsp. salt
1/2 tsp. celery seed
1/2 tsp. pickling spices
1/2 tsp. whole cloves
1 (3-inch) stick cinnamon

PREPARATION

Cut the unpeeled cucumbers, crosswise into 1/4-inch slices. Place them in a large crock or heavy enameled pot. Combine the lime and water and pour over the cucumber slices. Let stand, covered, 24 hours. Rinse and drain the cucumbers at least 8 times under cold running water. Return the cucumber slices to a clean pot. Cover with cold water; let stand, uncovered, 3 hours. Drain. Place the cucumbers in a large pot. Combine the vinegar, sugar, and salt in a large saucepan. Tie the celery seed, spices, cloves, and cinnamon stick in a cheesecloth bag and add this to the pan. Heat to boiling; pour over the cucumbers. Cool, then cover and let stand 24 hours.

The next day, drain the cucumbers, transferring the liquid to a saucepan. Heat the liquid to boiling; reduce the heat. Gently simmer (do not boil) uncovered, 35 minutes. Remove the bag of spices. Place the pickles with the juices in sterilized jars while hot. Seal.

MAKES ABOUT 6 PINTS

JACK CARNEY'S OYSTER STUFFING

Ingredients:

1 cup celery, finely chopped
1/2 cup onion, chopped
1/2 cup butter
1 tsp. poultry seasoning or sage
1/2 tsp. salt
1/8 tsp. pepper
8 cups dry bread crumbs
3/4 – 1 cup chicken broth (or the reserved liquid from the oysters)
1 pint oysters, shucked, drained & chopped
OR 2 (8-oz.) cans whole oysters, drained and chopped

In a saucepan, cook celery and onion in butter until tender, but not brown. Remove from heat and stir in poultry seasoning or sage, salt, pepper, and oysters. Place the bread crumbs in a large mixing bowl. Add the oyster mixture. Drizzle with enough broth to moisten, tossing lightly.

USE TO STUFF ONE 10-POUND TURKEY

JAKE'S STEAKS

708 N. 2nd St. 314-621-8184 www.jakessteaks.com

PICKLED SHRIMP

Ingredients
1-1/2 bottles or 18 oz. dark beer
1 cup vinegar
1 cup brown sugar
1/2 cup pickling spice
1/2 Tbs. garlic
2 bay leaves
1 lb. cooked shrimp, peeled and deveined
2 lemons, sliced
6 dried red chiles
1 onion, sliced

Place shrimp, onion, lemon and chiles in a jar. Boil first six ingredients and pour over shrimp.

JIMMY'S ON THE PARK

706 DeMun Ave. 314-725-8585 www.jimmyscafe.com

CRASH CAKES

Ingredients
1/2 lb. crab
1/2 lb. salmon
1/2 lb. scallops
1/2 red pepper, diced
1/2 yellow pepper, diced
1 rib celery, diced
2 eggs
1/2 cup heavy cream
cayenne pepper
salt and pepper
cumin
garlic
dry mustard
thyme
4 cups fresh white breadcrumbs

PREPARATION

Pick through crab to remove shells. Dice scallops and salmon. Finely chop peppers and celery. Sauté lightly. Heat heavy cream and eggs. Stir until slightly thick. Add seasonings. Mix vegetables, seafood and cream together. Finish with breadcrumbs. Sauté one small crash cake to check seasonings, adjust to your taste.

SERVES 4

LORENZO'S TRATTORIA

1933 Edwards St. 314-773-2223

EGGPLANT ROLLS

Ingredients
1 medium eggplant, thinly sliced lengthwise
10-12 slices of prosciutto
2 cups ricotta cheese
1/2 cup parsley, chopped
1/2 cup chives, chopped
12 oz. mozzarella cheese
12 oz. basic tomato sauce
olive oil
salt and pepper to taste

PREPARATION

First mix together ricotta cheese, parsley, chives and salt and pepper. Set aside. Brush both sides of your thinly sliced eggplant with olive oil. Next, grill both sides. Remove from grill and place one piece of prosciutto on each piece of grilled eggplant. Place ricotta mixture on the wider end of the eggplant and then roll. Coat each roll with breadcrumbs. Sauté in the pan on medium heat until browned. Place 2 oz. of tomato sauce on each plate. Top with 2 eggplant rolls and mozzarella cheese. Bake until cheese is melted.

MAKES 10-12 ROLLS

MANGO AUTHENTIC PERUVIAN CUISINE

7307 Watson Rd. 314-752-8300

PAPA ALA HUANCAINA
PERUVIAN CHILLED POTATO SALAD

Ingredients
1 tsp. minced garlic
2 Tbs. vegetable oil
5 aji amarillos , Peruvian yellow pepper
1/2 lb. (1/4 kg) fresh white cheese
1 cup evaporated milk
freshly squeezed juice of 1/2 key lime
oil
6 boiled white potatoes
salt, pepper and 1/4 tsp. turmeric

For garnish presentation:
1 hard-boiled egg, sliced
black olive slices
chopped parsley
lettuce leaves

PREPARATION

Seed, devein and chop aji amarillos. In small skillet heat vegetable oil and sauté garlic, aji amarillo, and turmeric for about 3 minutes. In food processor blend garlic, cheese, evaporated milk and salt and pepper, adding just enough vegetable oil to give mixture a smooth, creamy consistency. Add key lime juice and blend for a few seconds more. Adjust seasoning to taste, adding salt if necessary.

To serve, garnish plate with lettuce leaves before serving chilled potatoes. Pour sauce over sliced potatoes and garnish with boiled egg slices and black olive slices.

SERVES 6

NIK'S PORTOBELLO MUSHROOM AND GARLIC HUMMUS

Ingredients
2-3 cups dried chickpeas
3 portobello mushroom heads
extra virgin olive oil
fresh minced garlic

PREPARATION

Soak dried chickpeas overnight. Drain the chickpeas and boil them in fresh water for 2 to 6 hours or until they can very easily be smashed with wooden spoon. Drain chickpeas right before you are ready to make the hummus. Cut up mushroom heads and sauté in fresh garlic and olive oil.

4 cups drained and boiled chickpeas
1 Tbs. mixed dried herbs (we suggest some basil, oregano, dried mustard)
2 Tbs. tahini
1/4 cup soy sauce (tamari)
1/4 cup lemon juice

Blend 4 cups prepared chickpeas, herbs, tahini, soy sauce and lemon juice in a food processor until smooth and color is consistent throughout the batch. Add the portobellos. They should be thoroughly cooked. Process only slightly, so that large pieces are recognizable. Stir mushrooms and garlic into hummus with a spoon (don't process with hummus). Add the olive oil that the mushrooms were cooked in, for moisture. Serve with chips, pita bread or romaine leaves.

O'LEARY'S

3828 S. Lindbergh Blvd. 314-842-7678

O'LEARY'S FRIED PICKLES

Ingredients
4 cups all purpose flour
2 qts. vegetable oil
2 Tbs. paprika
2 tsp. garlic powder
2 tsp. black pepper
1 tsp. white pepper
1/2 tsp. cayenne pepper
2 cups dill pickle slices, drained

PREPARATION

Heat vegetable oil to 350 degrees. Mix all dry ingredients. Dredge pickle slices in flour mixture. Fry in preheated oil for 3-5 minutes or until crisp. Drain pickles on paper towel and serve immediately with dipping sauce.

Dipping Sauce
1 cup medium salsa
2 cups ranch dressing

Mix thoroughly

CORNMEAL FRIED TOMATOES WITH FRESH BASIL MAYONNAISE

Ingredients
4 tomatoes, sliced 1/2 inch thick
2 cups flour

1 pt. milk and 1 egg for egg wash

For seasoned cornmeal:
2 cups cornmeal
2 cups flour
1 tsp. salt
1 pinch ground white pepper
3 cups lard or salad oil
1 lb. white cheddar cheese, shaved

PREPARATION

Dip tomato slices in flour, then egg wash, then flour, and then egg wash again. Dip in seasoned corn-meal. Fry in hot lard or oil until golden brown and crisp. Place on a pizza pan or cookie sheet and top with cheddar. Place in 350-degree oven to melt cheese.

Serve on a bed of shredded lettuce or mixed field greens. Serve with fresh basil mayonnaise. Garnish with diced tomato and basil leaves.

Basil Mayonnaise
Ingredients
4 egg yolks
1 Tbs. lemon juice
1 tsp. Dijon mustard
pinch of salt
3 Tbs. fresh basil, chopped
3 cups salad oil

In a mixing bowl place egg yolks, lemon juice, salt, Dijon and basil. Use a whisk to slowly whip in the oil until thick and firm.

PORT ST. LOUIS

OYSTERS ROCKEFELLER
OR MUSHROOM ROCKEFELLER

Ingredients
12 oysters
3 ribs celery, chopped fine
1 small onion, chopped fine
2 (6-8 oz.) boxes frozen chopped spinach, thawed
1/2 cup heavy cream
2 Tbs. Pernod

PREPARATION

Sauté celery and onion, then add spinach. Add cream and Pernod. Then add salt and pepper to taste. Spoon onto oysters and top with breadcrumbs and Parmesan cheese. Bake in oven at 400 degrees until brown. Serve hot.

**For variety, use fresh white mushrooms with the above ingredients.

SERVES 4

PROTZEL'S DELI

7608 Wydown Blvd. 314-721-4445

PROTZEL'S DELI KAMISH BREAD

Ingredients
1 cup non-trans fat or regular Crisco
1 cup sugar
4 large eggs
1 tsp. vanilla
4 cups flour
1 tsp. baking powder
1/2 cup chopped pecans
1/2 cup cinnamon and sugar mixture

PREPARATION

Mix sugar and eggs together, then add in all ingredients except flour. Mix well then add flour, a little bit at a time. Fold in nuts. This dough will be thick.

On an ungreased baking sheet, form 2 log-like shapes, 7 inches wide and about 2 inches high. Sprinkle with a good amount of cinnamon/sugar.

Bake at 350 degrees for about 35 minutes or until lightly golden brown. Take out of oven and cut cookies in 1/2-inch pieces. Lightly sprinkle with more cinnamon and sugar and turn on side and bake for 5 minutes or until lightly golden brown.

RED CEDAR INN

RED CEDAR INN COUNTRY CARROTS

Ingredients
8 cups carrots, sliced
1 Tbs. minced onion
1 tsp. sugar
1 cup ground onion
1 Tbs. bacon drippings
1 cup water from parboiled carrots
1 tsp. chicken base
1 Tbs. seasoning*
4 slices cooked, crumbled bacon

PREPARATION

Clean and slice carrots. Parboil carrots with minced onion and sugar in barely enough water to cover. Meanwhile fry bacon until crisp. Drain on absorbent paper. Sauté ground onion in bacon drippings, and then add water, chicken base, and seasoning powder. Continue cooking carrots until tender. To serve, top carrots with crumbled bacon.

*a good mixed seasoning like Lowry's.

SERVES 10-12

REDEL'S

SALMON CAKES

Ingredients
2 lb. salmon meat
2 cups breadcrumbs
6 eggs
1/3 cup mayonnaise
2 medium onions, ground
2 medium green peppers, ground
1/2 tsp. thyme
1/2 tsp. basil
1 Tbs. Old Bay seasoning
Lemon juice

PREPARATION

Poach salmon in water, lemon juice, and salt until firm. Remove from heat, de-bone and cool. Mix remaining ingredients with salmon in large bowl. Portion mixture into 3 oz. patties. Roll patties in breadcrumbs. Patties may be baked, deep fried or sautéed. (Recommend sauté.)

SERVES 3-4

SLAY'S

HUMMUS

Ingredients
1 gal. garbanzo beans
1 (8-oz.) jar tahini
1 qt. water
1-1/2 cups lemon juice
4 oz. garlic
1 Tbs. salt

PREPARATION

Grind garbanzo beans, and then add the rest of the ingredients in the mixer. Add water for smoothness as necessary.

SMITH & SLAY'S
GONE BUT NOT FORGOTTEN

DAVID SLAY'S MACARONI & CHEESE

Ingredients
1 (16 oz.) pkg. elbow macaroni
1/2 lb. shredded white Vermont cheddar
1 qt. cream
4 oz. butter, melted
4 oz. flour
salt and pepper
1 cup breadcrumbs

PREPARATION

Bring elbow macaroni to a boil, about 12 minutes. Drain in a colander. Bring the quart of cream to a slow simmer. Combine the 4 oz. of flour and melted butter together into a roux. Mix in salt and pepper to taste. Add cheese to cream mixture. Mix cream together with noodles. Put in individual gratins or casserole dish. Sprinkle liberally with breadcrumbs and bake in 350-degree oven until breadcrumbs are browned, about 7 minutes.

BROCCOLI & CHEESE STRUDEL

Ingredients
2 large onions (3-4 cups)
12 cups broccoli, chopped stems and tops
salt and pepper to taste
4 cups breadcrumbs
4 cups shredded cheddar cheese
juice from 1 lemon
4 eggs
phyllo dough
sesame seeds

PREPARATION

Cook onions in 4-5 Tbs. butter until tender. Add broccoli; cook 8 minutes until bright green but firm. Add salt and pepper to taste. Add breadcrumbs and cheese. Add lemon juice, eggs and salt and pepper.

Brush phyllo dough with melted butter and place 4 sheets together. Place 4 equal portions onto the dough. Fold in sides and roll up. Place on greased cookie sheet. Brush with melted butter. Make 4 slits on top. Sprinkle with sesame seeds. Bake 25 minutes in 350-degree oven or until lightly browned.

EACH LOAF SERVES 3 SLICES

WHOLLY MACKEREL

403 Lafayette Center 636-265-3949

CRAB CAKES WITH
BRAZILIAN COCONUT CREAM

Ingredients
24 oz. lump or claw crabmeat
6 oz. mango
4 oz. yellow onion, diced
2 tsp. Worcestershire sauce
Salt and pepper
Japanese breadcrumbs
3 whole eggs
2 Tbs. Old Bay seasoning
4 oz. mayonnaise
olive oil

PREPARATION

Drain crabmeat, being careful not to shred meat. Peel and dice mango. (You can use prepared mango spears in a jar if you'd like.) Combine crabmeat, mango, and onion. Mix thoroughly. Season with Worcestershire, pinch of salt and pepper, and Old Bay seasoning. Mix mayonnaise into mixture. Add whole beaten eggs and mix thoroughly. Add breadcrumbs to desired consistency. When crab cakes are molded, the consistency should be compact. Heat skillet with olive oil and brown on each side; then put crab cakes in 500-degree oven for 10 minutes.

Brazilian Coconut Cream Ingredients
1 can coconut milk
1 oz. palm oil

Add coconut milk in skillet and reduce by half (cream will thicken when cooled). Once reduced, heat in skillet and add 1 oz. palm oil to color.

SERVES 4

SALADS

CLARKSVILLE STATION

901 S. Highway 79, Clarksville, MO 573-242-3838

CURRIED CHICKEN SALAD

Ingredients
3 lbs. cooked chicken breast, diced
4 Tbs. curry powder
2 cups pecans, chopped
1 cup bacon, cooked crispy and chopped
2 cups grapes, halved
3 cups mayonnaise
salt and pepper to taste

Cut the chicken into 1/2-inch cubes. Stir curry into the mayonnaise. Combine all ingredients and mix until evenly colored. Season with salt and pepper.

SERVES 5

CRAVINGS

8149 Big Bend Blvd. 314-961-3534

CURRIED CHICKEN SALAD

Ingredients
10 (5-oz.) boneless, skinless chicken breasts
1 (12-oz.) can unsweetened coconut milk
3 Tbs. garlic, minced
5 slices of fresh ginger root
1-1/2 Tbs. yellow curry powder
1-1/2 tsp. coriander
1 tsp. salt
3 tsp. soy sauce

Place all the ingredients except the chicken in a food processor and process until well blended. Place the chicken breasts in an appropriate-size pan and pour the processed marinade over the top. Marinate in the refrigerator for 1-2 hours (no longer). Remove the chicken breasts from the marinade and place flat on a baking sheet. Bake in a preheated 375-degree oven for 12 minutes or until the juices run clear when you pierce the thickest part. Remove from the oven and chill. Dice into 1/2-inch pieces.

Ingredients for Chicken Salad:
2 stalks fresh celery, cut into 1/4 inch slices
3/4 cup red onion, finely chopped
1 cup curry mayonnaise
1-1/2 cups plump raisins

Add the diced chicken to a bowl with all of the above ingredients. Mix thoroughly and chill. Place on a bed of baby lettuces that are lightly tossed in your favorite herb vinaigrette. Place one cup of curried chicken salad on top of greens. Sprinkle with sliced almonds.

SERVES 10 – 12

LOBSTER WEST INDIES SALAD

Ingredients
2 lbs. lobster meat, raw
1 Tbs. curry powder
2 oz. peanut oil or sunflower oil
2 tsp. red onion, diced small
2 tsp. red pepper, diced small
2 tsp. green pepper, diced small
2 Tbs. green onion, sliced
2 Tbs. Coco-Lopez cream of coconut
2 tsp. crème de banana liquor
7 Tbs. mayonnaise
3 Tbs. red apple, peeled and diced
1/4 tsp. cayenne pepper
1 Tbs. cracked black pepper
1 tsp. salt
Garnish Ingredients: kiwi, orange and red bell peppers, leaf lettuce

PREPARATION

Cut the lobster meat into approximately 1/4-inch dice. Heat oil and add the lobster meat and curry powder. Cook and stir until lobster meat has become opaque. Add the red onion and bell peppers. Quickly stir and remove from heat. Place this mixture in the refrigerator until well chilled. Add the remaining ingredients and chill overnight. Garnish with lettuce leaves, peeled and sliced kiwi and orange and red bell pepper.

Note: The lobster can easily be substituted with shrimp, scallops, or crabmeat.

SERVES 8

GIOVANNI'S LITTLE PLACE

14560 Manchester Rd. 636-227-7230

TOMATO AND MOZZARELLA SALAD

Ingredients
3-4 tomatoes
2 balls of mozzarella cheese
6 Tbs. extra virgin olive oil
4 Tbs. balsamic vinegar
salt and freshly ground pepper
fresh basil sprigs
1/4 oz. oregano

PREPARATION

Cut the tomatoes lengthwise into even slices. Cut each ball of mozzarella cheese into 6 even slices. Alternate the tomato and mozzarella cheese slices on individual plates, fanning them out a little to make an attractive pattern. Whisk together the olive oil and vinegar with salt and pepper to taste. Drizzle a touch of oregano and the dressing over the salad and garnish with basil.

GP AGOSTINO'S

15846 Manchester Rd. 636-391-5480

GIAN-PAUL SALAD

Ingredients
1 head romaine lettuce
5 oz. salami, diced
5 oz. Mortadella
2-3 oz. iceberg lettuce
1 ripe tomato, diced
3 oz. Fontina cheese, diced
1 1/2 oz. dry Roquefort cheese crumbles
1 Tbs. salt
Pinch freshly ground pepper
4 anchovy filets, chopped
1/2 cup olive oil
1/8 cup red wine vinegar
1/4 cup blue cheese salad dressing
2 oz. red cabbage, sliced thin

PREPARATION

When ready to serve, toss all the ingredients together with oil, vinegar and blue cheese dressing.

SERVES 6

CAESAR SALAD

Caesar Dressing Ingredients
3 eggs + 1 yolk
3/4 cup fresh lemon juice
15 cloves garlic
2 cups Parmesan cheese
2 Tbs. whole grain mustard
1 tsp. Tabasco
3/4 cup anchovies
1-1/2 Tbs. black pepper
2-1/2 cups extra virgin olive oil

PREPARATION

Mix together all ingredients except the olive oil. Slowly add olive oil.

Caesar Croutons Ingredients
2 loaves French bread
2 cups olive oil
1/2 cup diced anchovies
1/2 cup minced garlic
1 cup Parmesan

PREPARATION

Cut French bread in half through the middle, and in half again through the top. Then slice entire loaf into 1-1/2 inch thick croutons. Bake croutons on sheet pan in 400-degree oven for about 10 minutes, or until croutons are crisp.

In small saucepot add olive oil, diced anchovies and garlic. Bring mixture to a boil on low heat and cook until anchovies are dissolved in the oil. Pour hot oil over baked croutons in large mixing bowl and sprinkle with 1 cup Parmesan. Toss with metal spoon.

JIMMY'S ON THE PARK

706 DeMun Ave. 314-725-8585 www.jimmyscafe.com

BISTRO WILTED SALAD

Ingredients
Vinaigrette
1/4 lb. pancetta bacon
1/8 cup white vinegar
1/8 cup sugar
1 tsp. cracked black pepper

Salad
2 cups baby spinach
1 Tbs. pine nuts
2 Tbs. sun-dried cranberries
2 Tbs. Gorgonzola cheese

PREPARATION

Chop pancetta into small chunks. In a sauté skillet, brown pancetta then add vinegar, sugar and cracked pepper. With the vinaigrette still warm, toss the spinach until wilted, yet still crisp. Once tossed, finish with cranberries, pine nuts and Gorgonzola.

MODESTO
TAPAS BAR & RESTAURANT

5257 Shaw Ave. 314-772-8272

SALPICON DE MARISCOS
(MARINATED SEAFOOD SALAD)

Ingredients
1 lb. monkfish
1 lb. squid, tubes and tentacles
1 lb. rock shrimp
1 lb. lump crabmeat
juice of 10 limes
1/2 cup cilantro, chopped
2 cups extra virgin olive oil
salt to taste

PREPARATION

Add all ingredients to bowl and mix well. Refrigerate for 2 hours. Serve chilled with fried capers and lemon wedges.

SERVES 10-12 AS A TAPAS

THE PASTA HOUSE CO.

1143 Macklind Ave. 314-535-6644

THE PASTA HOUSE CO. SPECIAL SALAD

1 head iceberg lettuce
1/3 head romaine lettuce
1 cup artichoke hearts, not marinated
1 cup red onions, sliced
1 cup pimentos, diced
2/3 cup olive oil
1/3 cup Regina wine vinegar
1 tsp. salt
1/4 tsp. black pepper
2/3 cup Parmigiano cheese, freshly grated

PREPARATION

Wash the iceberg and romaine lettuce, allowing all the water to drain completely. Place in refrigerator to chill. When lettuce is well chilled, remove from refrigerator. Split the head of iceberg lettuce in half, pulling the heart of lettuce out of both halves and breaking into small pieces. Do not use a knife on lettuce. Only separate the rest of the iceberg; it will break up when tossed. Tear the romaine lettuce- each leaf into 3 sections. Place both kinds of lettuce into a large bowl.

Drain artichoke hearts well; measure and add to lettuce. Do not use marinated artichoke hearts. Peel and slice red onion; drain and dice pimentos. (Drain pimentos completely or salad will turn red.) Measure the onions and pimentos and add to lettuce.

Add olive oil, vinegar, salt, pepper and toss. Add Parmigiano cheese. Toss until mixed completely and serve.

SERVES 4

PORTABELLA

15 N. Central Ave. 314-725-6588

GRILLED ASPARAGUS AND PORTOBELLO MUSHROOM WITH BALSAMIC VINAIGRETTE

Ingredients

24 medium asparagus spears
6 (medium to large) portobello mushrooms
1 Tbs. shallots, chopped
1 cup olive oil
1/2 cup balsamic vinegar
1 tsp. each salt and pepper

PREPARATION

Cut stems off of asparagus and discard. Add asparagus to a pot of boiling salt water and cook until *al dente*. Remove from boiling water and place in an ice bath, until cooled. Coat with olive oil and salt and pepper and grill until tender.

Remove 3/4 of stem from mushroom; discard. Clean mushroom with a damp rag. Place in a mixing bowl and toss with olive oil, balsamic vinegar, salt, pepper and shallots. Place on grill and cook until tender on both sides. (About 8-10 minutes.)

Balsamic Vinaigrette Ingredients

2 tsp. Dijon mustard
1 tsp. shallots, chopped
2 Tbs. basil, chopped
4 oz. balsamic vinegar
12 oz. extra virgin olive oil
1 Tbs. each salt and pepper

PREPARATION

While whisking mustard, shallot, basil and vinegar in a mixing bowl, slowly add in olive oil so that an emulsion is created. Adjust seasoning with salt and pepper. Cover and refrigerate.

STIR CRAZY

10598 Old Olive Street Rd. 314-569-9300

MANGO SALMON SALAD

Ingredients
8 (6-oz.) salmon filets
2 lbs. baby lettuce mix
1-1/2 lbs. mango, diced
1 lb. red onions, sliced
16 Tbs. toasted almond slices
1 cup Japanese basting sauce
2-1/2 cups ginger soy vinaigrette (see recipe)
8 Tbs. toasted almond slices (for garnish)

PREPARATION

In a large mixing bowl, mix the baby lettuce, mango, red onions, almond slices and dressing (mix dressing well before adding). Mix until salad is evenly dressed. Divide the salad mixture and mound in the middle of the serving bowls. Place the salmon filets into shallow baking pan; baste each filet with Japanese basting sauce. Bake at 500 degrees for approximately 6 minutes. Lean the cooked salmon against the lettuce mix and sprinkle each salad with 1 Tbs. of toasted almond slices.

SERVES 8

Ginger Soy Vinaigrette Ingredients
1/2 oz. fresh ginger, peeled and minced
1/4 oz. fresh garlic, minced
1-1/2 oz. soy sauce
6 oz. rice vinegar
5 oz. sugar
1 tsp. salt
1/2 oz. mustard
1/2 oz. sesame oil
6 oz. canola oil

Combine all ingredients except for the sesame oil and canola oil and mix with hand mixer (or in blender) for 1 minute. Mix the sesame oil and canola oil together. Slowly drizzle the oils into the mixture of other ingredients while continuing to mix. Do not add too quickly or dressing will separate.

YIELDS 2-1/2 CUPS

TOMATILLO MEXICAN GRILL

7931 Forsyth 314-726-6688

TACO SALAD

Ingredients
4 (10-inch) flour tortillas

Salad:
2 cups cooked black beans or 1 can black beans, heated
1 head iceberg lettuce, shredded or finely chopped
your choice of grilled chicken or grilled steak
shredded Monterey jack cheese, sour cream, diced tomatoes

Salsa Vinaigrette:
3/4 cup olive oil
1/4 cup rice wine vinegar
1/4 cup honey
1/4 cup fresh cilantro, chopped
1 Tbs. cumin
1 tsp. salt
1/2 tsp. black pepper
1/4 cup cooked corn
2 Tbs. Tabasco or hot sauce
1/2 cup chopped tomatoes

PREPARATION

In a large pot, heat vegetable oil and deep fry each of the tortillas. Mix salad ingredients together. For the salsa vinaigrette, mix all ingredients in food processor or blender.
Toss the salad with the vinaigrette and place in taco salad shell. Top with sour cream and cheese.

SERVES 4

MAIN DISHES

609 AND U RESTAURANT AND LOUNGE

609 Eastgate Ave. 314-721-9168

PANKO-CRUSTED HALIBUT, ENGLISH PEA RISOTTO AND SHRIMP AND CARROT NAGE

Ingredients
4 (6-oz.) halibut filets
1 bag panko breadcrumbs
1 Tbs. butter
1 Tbs. oil

PREPARATION

Add oil and butter in a large sauté pan and put on high heat. Season fish with salt and pepper and put flesh-side down into panko. Once butter has melted, place fish panko-side down in sauté pan. Once panko has browned, turn fish and place into a 350-degree oven for 5-10 minutes, depending on thickness of the fish.

English Pea Risotto
Ingredients
2 cups Arborio rice
1 cup white wine
3 cups chicken broth
1/2 small yellow onion, diced
2 cups English peas
2 cups spinach
1 Tbs. butter
2 Tbs. Parmesan cheese

In a pot of boiling water, add 3/4 of the peas and the spinach. Remove after 30 seconds and put into ice water. Drain; puree in a blender. In a large saucepot, sweat the onions in oil. Add the rice and the white wine. Stir with a wooden spoon until wine is completely evaporated. Add the chicken stock in three parts, stirring constantly. When the rice is tender, add the pea puree and half of the remaining peas. Turn off the heat and add in butter and Parmesan cheese. Season with salt and pepper.

Shrimp and Carrot Nage
Ingredients
2 lbs. shrimp shells
1 gallon water
1/2 cup tomato paste
1/4 cup carrot juice
1/2 lb. butter
1/4 cup heavy cream

In an 8-quart stockpot, heat oil to smoking. Add shrimp shells and stir occasionally until shells are pink. Add tomato paste and water and simmer for one hour. Strain shells and reduce sauce until thick. Add carrot juice and cream and reduce until thick. Turn off the heat and slowly whisk in butter. Keep warm until serving.

SERVES 4

ADRIANA'S

5101 Shaw Ave. 314-773-3833

SICILIAN SPINACH PIE

Ingredients
1 cup onion, chopped
2 Tbs. olive oil
1-1/4 cup breadcrumbs
1/2 cup Romano cheese, grated
1 cup tomato basil sauce or 1 cup of your favorite red sauce (no meat)
3 (10-oz.) boxes frozen spinach, chopped
1-1/2 cups ricotta cheese
6 eggs
1 tsp. salt
1/2 tsp. black pepper
1 or 2 pinches red pepper flakes (optional)

PREPARATION

Sauté onion in the olive oil until it is transparent. In a large bowl, combine all ingredients plus the sautéed onions. Mix well by hand. Spray 10-inch pie pan with no-stick cooking spray. Place mixture in pan and form into pie shape. Bake at 350 degrees for 1 hour 15 minutes. It should be firm to the touch. Cut into wedges. Serve with extra red sauce and top with grated cheese. *Mangia bene!*

AL BAKER'S RESTAURANT

GONE BUT NOT FORGOTTEN

LINGUINE AL PORCINO

Ingredients
1 Tbs. olive oil
1 Tbs. green onion, chopped
1 tsp. garlic, chopped
6 oz. chicken stock
2 medium Italian tomatoes, crushed
2 Tbs. juice from Italian tomatoes
1 Tbs. fresh basil, chopped
1/4 tsp. crushed red pepper
3 medium sun-dried tomatoes
1 Tbs. fresh mushrooms, chopped

PREPARATION

Boil sun-dried tomatoes and mushrooms in water for 1 minute prior to use. Sauté garlic in oil. Add green onions, sauté for 1 minute. Add chicken stock, tomatoes, juice, red pepper, sun-dried tomatoes, and mushrooms.

Bring to boil, then reduce to a simmer. Reduce sauce by one-third and add chopped basil. Combine with pasta. Toss and serve.

ANNIE GUNN'S

16806 Chesterfield Airport Rd. 636-532-7684

GRILLED PEPPERED BEEF TENDERLOIN
WITH A CHANTERELLE MUSHROOM CABERNET TOASTED GARLIC SAUCE AND WHIPPED YUKON GOLD POTATOES

Ingredients
2 (10-oz.) Beef Tenderloin filets
3 Tbs. fresh, cracked black pepper

Chanterelle Mushroom Sauce
2 minced garlic cloves
1 Tbs. fresh thyme
3 oz. Cabernet
3 oz. brown veal stock
cracked pepper to taste
kosher salt to taste
2 Tbs. whole unsalted butter

Whipped Yukon Gold Potatoes
2 lbs. peeled Yukon Gold potatoes
2 cups heavy cream
8 oz. unsalted butter
kosher salt to taste
white pepper to taste

PREPARATION

Have the butcher cut center filets of beef tenderloin. Roll edges of the filet in the pepper and season edges with salt. Hold until ready to serve. Grill to desired degrees of doneness.

Sauté mushrooms in a skillet with oil until tender. Add minced garlic and allow to lightly brown. Deglaze skillet with wine and reduce by three-fourths. Add brown veal stock and reduce by half. Add fresh thyme and finish with butter. Season with salt and pepper to taste. Keep warm until ready to serve.

Put diced tomatoes into a stockpot with lukewarm water to cover and bring to a boil. Reduce to a simmer and skim the foam off the top. Cook until tender. Heat cream and butter in a saucepan while potatoes are cooking. Drain water from cooked potatoes and put through a sieve. Add the warm butter cream mixture and season with salt and pepper. Whip potatoes vigorously. Place a ladle of mushroom sauce on plate and top with steak and mashed potatoes. Include a seasonal vegetable to finish.

ASTORIA

12949 Olive Blvd. 314-878-7711

BEEF STROGANOFF

Ingredients
8 oz. beef tenderloin, sliced into thin strips
1 Tbs. olive oil
1-1/2 oz. vodka
2 oz. mushrooms, sliced thin
2 oz. onion, sliced thin
1 tsp. sugar
1 tsp. spicy Dijon mustard
salt and pepper to taste
1/2 cup heavy cream
1 large potato, sliced into thin strips and fried

PREPARATION

Add olive oil to a hot pan; then add the sliced beef. Allow the meat to become browned and then deglaze the pan with the vodka. (Be careful to pour away from the fire). Add the mushrooms and onions and cook briefly. Then add sugar, Dijon mustard, salt, and pepper and allow it to cook, stirring constantly, for about three minutes. Add the cream and cook for about five minutes or until the cream has reduced into a thick rich sauce. Finish by stirring to coat the meat. To finish this dish in the classic Russian way, add thinly sliced fried potatoes directly on top.

ROASTED MARINATED SALMON

Ingredients
2 lb. salmon filets
1/4 cup olive oil
4 cloves fresh garlic, chopped
1/2 tsp. sea salt
1/4 tsp. black pepper, freshly ground
peel of 1/2 lemon, cut into very fine strips or chopped
fresh herbs (a sprig or two), chopped

PREPARATION

This is a simple preparation that follows the Italian esthetic of fine ingredients combined with a light and subtle hand, with the aim being to let the fish itself shine and to avoid distractions of flavor.

First, find the freshest fish. The variety of fish is always a distant second consideration. If salmon is not available, substitute any light- to medium-fleshed fish, such as cod, wahoo or striped bass, or any other fish for that matter. (The exception is tuna, as drying out can be a problem. You may then adjust seasoning and cooking times for a tasty result.)

Rinse the fish and pat dry; then cut it into serving pieces. Combine the other ingredients in a small bowl and mix well. You can be more liberal with milder herbs like Italian parsley or basil, but use less of rosemary or tarragon. (A vegetable peeler can be used in place of a zester for the lemon.) Coat the fish with the marinade; refrigerate, covered, for one to four hours.

Roast the fish in an oven preheated to 425 degrees for 8-12 minutes, or until just done (opaque all the way through). Cooking times will vary with the type and thickness of the fish. Fennel, prepared hot or cold, makes an excellent accompaniment. A bulb or two, sliced thinly, can be sautéed with julienne red bell pepper in a little olive oil, with a touch of garlic, salt and pepper. Sliced fennel also makes a lovely salad with sliced mushrooms, fresh lemon juice and olive oil.

SERVES 4

BARTOLINO'S

2524 Hampton Ave. 314-644-2266

PASTA DI GIUBILEO

Ingredients
1 lb. penne pasta
1/3 cup toasted pine nuts
1 cup fresh spinach, packed
1/4 cup sun-dried tomatoes, julienne, in olive oil
1/2 cup extra virgin olive oil
3 cloves fresh garlic, finely chopped
1/3 cup chicken stock
1/2 tsp. crushed red pepper
2 Tbs. butter
1 cup Bartolino's marinara sauce
5 leaves fresh basil, coarsely chopped

PREPARATION

Cook pasta according to directions. In a medium skillet, sauté garlic and crushed red pepper in olive oil until lightly browned. Add sun-dried tomatoes, chicken stock, butter, marinara sauce, basil and spinach. Cook on medium heat until heated. Toss with cooked pasta and put in serving bowl. Top with pine nuts.

BELLA CITTA

GONE BUT NOT FORGOTTEN

LINGUINI CON VONGOLE

Ingredients
linguini, measured for serving
garlic, chopped
cracked black pepper
ocean clam stock
ocean clams
tomatoes, chopped
fresh basil, oregano, parsley
1-1/2 oz. Pernod
1 oz. butter
Asiago cheese

PREPARATION

Open clams and save juices. Boil linguini to *al dente*. Blanch clams with water and clam juices. Chop clams, garlic, tomatoes, basil, oregano and parsley. Sauté clams in 1 oz. butter and garlic, adding chopped herbs and tomatoes; add Pernod. Strain linguini and add to clams. Add cracked black pepper and toss. Serve with freshly grated Asiago. Clam, linguini and tomato amounts vary to personal taste.

LOBSTER RISOTTO WITH GRILLED SCALLOPS

Ingredients
3 Tbs. olive oil
2 Tbs. garlic, chopped
1/4 cup leeks, chopped
1/4 cup onions, chopped
1 cup Arborio rice
2 cups lobster stock
1 cup white wine
1/4 cup mascarpone (Italian cream cheese)
1/4 cup Parmesan cheese
1/2 lb. lobster claw meat, cooked
1/4 cup chopped basil
salt and pepper to taste
scallops

PREPARATION

In a large stockpot, bring wine and lobster base to a boil. Using another large stockpot, add leeks, onion, and garlic to heated olive oil.

Fold rice into the leek, onion and garlic mixture. Stir in the boiling liquid, enough to cover rice. Continue adding small amounts of boiling liquid as it is absorbed by the rice, until all liquid has been combined into rice mixture.

Turn heat off. Fold in both cheeses and lobster. Season with salt and pepper to taste. Add chopped basil. Serve on platter with grilled scallops.

SERVES 4-6

OKRA GUMBO

Roux Ingredients
1/2 lb. margarine and 2 cups flour

Cook and stir over low flame to peanut butter brown.

Ingredients
4 cups onion
1 cup green pepper
2/3 cup scallions
6 lbs. frozen sliced okra

Cook over medium flame, stirring often, until the green peppers turn an olive green color.

Ingredients
2 Tbs. garlic
6 bay leaves
3 tsp. thyme
1/4 tsp. cayenne (or to taste)
3 Tbs. lemon juice
20 whole allspice
2 Tbs. salt
4 Tbs. wet chicken base
2-1/2 tsp. black pepper
16 whole cloves
1/2 tsp. nutmeg

Add to previous mixture, mix well and continue to cook for 10 minutes.

Ingredients
1 gal. water
3 cups diced tomatoes
6 gumbo crabs, split

Add to mixture, mix well, and bring to a boil, then simmer for approximately 2 hours, stirring often.

Ingredients
2 lbs. peeled 40/50 count shrimp

Add shrimp 5 minutes before serving. Serve in shallow soup bowls with a spoonful of cooked rice and crusty French bread.

BOBBY'S RESTAURANT

GONE BUT NOT FORGOTTEN

RED BEANS AND RICE

Ingredients
10 cups large red kidney beans
4 cups onion, chopped
2 cups green pepper, chopped
4 Tbs. diced garlic
3 Tbs. salt
1-1/2 tsp. black pepper
6 bay leaves
1-1/2 tsp. thyme
1/2 tsp. basil
2 lbs. cubed pork butt
2 lbs. andouille sausage

Soak the red beans in cold water for 10-12 hours. Drain the water from the beans. Add the onions, green pepper, garlic, pork butt, andouille sausage and the rest of the spices. Cover with cold water. Bring to a boil, reduce heat and simmer for 3 hours, stirring frequently. When the beans are soft, serve over rice with fresh scallions.

SERVES 16

BRANDT'S MARKET & CAFÉ

6525 Delmar Ave. 314-727-3663

CARIBBEAN BANANA-RUM FISH

Ingredients
4 white fish fillets

Sauce
3 ripe bananas
2 fresh jalapeño peppers
1-1/2 tsp. garlic, minced
1-1/2 tsp. ginger, minced
1 can coconut milk
1 cup fresh tomato, finely chopped
1/2 cup spiced rum
Vegetables, including red and yellow peppers, onion, tomato, and any other vegetable of your choice

Puree the first 5 sauce ingredients in a blender; then add tomato and spiced rum and set aside. Slice the vegetables.

Pan-sear the fish fillets in approximately 1-2 Tbs. olive oil for about 2 minutes per side, depending on thickness. Add sauce and vegetable medley and simmer until tender. Place fish on a dish, cover with sauce and vegetables on top, and garnish with slices of banana.

Traditionally this dish is served with curried coconut rice: rice cooked in coconut milk with curry seasoning to taste.

SERVES 4

CAFÉ BALABAN

405 N. Euclid Ave. 314-361-8085

TENDERLOIN OF BEEF WITH CAPTAIN MORGAN RUM SAUCE

Ingredients
3 medium yellow onions, julienne
2 oz. olive oil
1 cup balsamic vinegar
4 oz. honey
1 cup Captain Morgan Rum
1 cup veal stock
1 cup toasted pine nuts
4 cups shiitake mushrooms, julienne
2 oz. olive oil
1 cup heavy cream

PREPARATION

Over high heat, sauté onions in 2 oz. olive oil until they start to carmelize. Add vinegar and honey and reduce until almost dry. Add veal stock and cream, and reduce until slightly thickened.

In a separate pan, sauté mushrooms in 2 oz. olive oil. Add rum. (Be careful, it is inflammable.) Add reserved onion mixture. Heat through and add pine nuts. Cook beef tenderloin to desired temperature. Serve sauce over meat.

CAFÉ DE FRANCE

7517 Forsyth Blvd. 314-678-0200 www.saucecafe.com/cafedefrance

SALMON ROULADE EN CROUTE WITH ORANGE GINGER BEURRE BLANC

Salmon Roulade Ingredients

1-1/2 lb. fresh salmon filet, skinned, and pin bones removed
1/2 lb. fresh spinach, washed and picked clean
3/4 lb. Brie cheese, rind removed, and sliced thick
1 lb. Scallop Mousse (*see recipe)
1 sheet puff pastry (lightly flavored and rolled)
1/2 lemon
salt and pepper
melted butter
egg wash

PREPARATION

Split salmon with a sharp knife down center of filet, until approx. 1/4-inch from bottom, as if making an upside down "T". Horizontally cut from previous mark to either side, yet avoid cutting all the way through. Spread out salmon filet on top of plastic wrap. Cover top of salmon with plastic wrap. Lightly pound filet until approx. 1/4 inch thick. Remove top layer of plastic wrap. Lightly salt and pepper pounded filet, and then squeeze 1/2 lemon over entire filet. Spread scallop mousse from one end to the other. Place whole spinach leaves over entire filet. Lightly spread Brie slices over spinach. From one end, roll salmon into a tight cylinder, overlapping as many times as necessary. Place salmon roulade in the center of a puff pastry sheet. Wrap salmon from one end to the other in a tight roll. Preheat the oven to 375 degrees. Place salmon on buttered cooking sheet. Brush egg wash over entire roulade. Bake for 15 to 20 minutes on the top rack of the oven.

Scallop Mousse Ingredients

5 oz. sea or bay scallops (if sea scallops, remove muscle)
2-1/2 oz. 40% or heavy whipping cream
1 egg
salt and pepper to taste, and/or lemon juice

Process ingredients in food processor or blender until smooth.

Orange Ginger Beurre Blanc Ingredients

2 Tbs. fresh shallots, minced
1 Tbs. fresh ginger, minced
1 tsp. olive oil
1 orange, halved
1 cup white wine
1/2 cup Triple Sec
2/3 lb. whole butter
1/2 cup heavy cream (40% or more)
1 Tbs. lemon juice
salt and pepper to taste

In a saucepan (stainless steel preferable) sweat shallots and ginger in olive oil until translucent. Deglaze pan with orange juice, white wine and Triple Sec. Reduce by half. Add heavy cream. Bring to a low boil until sides of the pan start to brown. Add butter in small pieces (never add too much at once) while whisking continuously, until sauce starts to thicken. Remove from heat, strain, and serve immediately. Yields: 1-1/2 cups

CUNETTO HOUSE OF PASTA

5453 Magnolia Ave. 314-781-1135 www.cunetto.com

SPAGHETTI CON BROCCOLI

Ingredients
1 lb. spaghetti
24 oz. half and half
1/2 stick butter
3/4 -1 cup Parmesan cheese, freshly grated
1/2 lb. broccoli flowerets
1 cup mushrooms, sliced
1/4 cup parsley, minced
1 Tbs. black pepper
2 tsp. salt
1–1- 1/2 tsp. fresh garlic, minced

PREPARATION

Combine cream, butter, seasoning, mushrooms, parsley, and broccoli in saucepan over medium heat. Bring to a boil. Add cooked and drained spaghetti. Reduce over medium heat until cream sauce clings to the spaghetti. Remove from heat and toss in Parmesan cheese, small amounts at a time, until desired consistency is achieved.

SERVES 4

DEL PIETRO'S

5625 Hampton Ave. 314-531-1700

CHICKEN SPEDINI WITH PORTOBELLO MUSHROOMS

Portobello Ingredients
2 portobello mushrooms
extra virgin olive oil
salt and fresh ground pepper

Chicken Ingredients
2 boneless chicken breasts, skinned
1 cup breadcrumbs
salt and freshly ground pepper
2 Tbs. fresh Italian parsley, chopped
1/4 cup fresh Parmigiano cheese, grated
1/2 tsp. minced garlic
1/2 cup Del Pietro's salad dressing
1/2 fresh lemon, squeezed
splash of white wine
dash of balsamic vinegar

PREPARATION

Marinate cut chicken pieces in salad dressing, lemon juice and white wine for 1 hour.

Brush portobello mushrooms with olive oil and season with salt and pepper. Bake or broil on medium heat about 3 minutes or until tender. Remove from heat.

Skewer chicken and coat with breadcrumbs, cheese, garlic, parsley, salt, and pepper. Grill on medium high heat for about 10 minutes, turning to keep from burning the bread crumbs. Remove chicken from skewer and arrange with portobello mushrooms. Top with a dash of balsamic vinegar.

SERVES 2

VEAL FONTINA

Ingredients

1-1/2 lbs. veal, cut into 12 pieces and pounded into scallopine
1 cup flour
1 cup mushrooms, sliced medium
3 tsp. olive oil
1/2 stick butter
1 tsp. garlic
1 cup dry white wine
2 cups veal broth
1/4 lb. Fontina cheese, sliced thin
salt and pepper
2 tsp. chopped parsley

PREPARATION

Season scallopine with salt and pepper and flour lightly, shaking off excess. In a heated large skillet, put the olive oil and 1 tsp. butter. When the oil and butter are hot, place the veal in the skillet. Sear veal quickly on both sides. Remove from pan and place on a large platter.

To the same skillet add garlic, mushrooms and parsley. Sauté for one minute. Add the white wine and let reduce by half. After the wine has been reduced, add veal broth and let it reduce by two thirds; season with salt and pepper to taste. Then turn off heat and add the remaining butter to sauce. Stir until butter has dissolved and sauce has become creamy. Set aside.

Place one slice of cheese on each piece of veal. Cover with the sauce and place in oven on low heat to melt the cheese. When cheese has melted, top with chopped parsley and serve.

SERVES 4

DOMINIC'S TRATTORIA

200 S. Brentwood 314-863-4567 www.dominicsrestaurant.com

PETTI DI POLLO ALLA GINA
CHICKEN BREAST ALLA GINA

Ingredients
4 pcs. chicken breast
3 Tbs. virgin olive oil
1 Tbs. chopped parsley
4 Tbs. chicken stock
3 oz. prosciutto ham, diced
1/2 cup flour
3 Tbs. butter
1 oz. dry white wine
3 oz. Fontina cheese
4 Tbs. tomato sauce

PREPARATION

Skin and remove bone from four pieces of chicken breast. Slice into thin cutlets and flatten the slices as much as possible. The thinner the slices, the more delicate the dish will become. Coat slices lightly with flour. Then brown them delicately on each side, using olive oil and butter heated together in a skillet. Season the slices with salt and pepper. Coat each one with a light layer of Fontina cheese and finely diced prosciutto ham. Add tomato sauce, chicken stock and dry white wine.

Transfer chicken and sauce onto an oven-safe pan, and then put the pan into a slow oven at 325 degrees until the cheese has melted and the sauce has slightly thickened.

Serve each slice of chicken breast on a hot serving dish with the sauce poured over each slice of chicken. Serve on same plate green peas, mushrooms, asparagus, and mashed potatoes, or whichever vegetables you prefer; these are just what I suggest. Sprinkle the parsley over the chicken and enjoy.

SERVES 4

DUFF'S RESTAURANT

389 N. Euclid Ave. 314-361-0522 www.dineatduffs.com

BOW THAI

Ingredients
1 qt. Rice Dream
1 (10-oz.) can coconut milk
4 lemongrass stalks, minced
4 lime leaves, julienne
1 Tbs. galangal, chopped
1 Tbs. garlic, minced
1 Tbs. ginger, mined
1 Tbs. lime juice
1/4 cup shallots, minced
1/4 cup chili sauce for chicken
chopped stems from 1 bunch cilantro
(chop and reserve leaves for finishing dish)
arrowroot powder

PREPARATION

Simmer all ingredients except cilantro stems and arrowroot powder for 30 minutes, then strain. Bring to a boil. Mix 2 Tbs. arrowroot powder with 2 Tbs. water and whisk mixture into sauce to thicken. Cook 1 lb. bow tie pasta in boiling water until *al dente*.

Ingredients
1 lb. peeled and deveined shrimp
1/2 lb. sugar snap peas
4 oz. shiitake mushrooms, sliced
1 red bell pepper, julienne

Add ingredients to sauce and simmer shrimp and vegetables in sauce until shrimp are just done; then add pasta and chopped cilantro. Serve in your favorite pasta bowl.

* These items can be found at Asian food stores. You can add other fish, shellfish, and chicken or add lots of vegetables for a vegetarian dinner.

SERVES 4

GORKHALI CHICKEN
CLASSIC TENDER CHICKEN CURRY WITH HIMALAYAN HERBS

Ingredients
2 lbs. chicken, dark and light, skinned, boned, cut into 1/2-inch cubes
2 cups onion, chopped
1 tsp. cumin powder
1 tsp. curry powder
1/2 tsp. chili powder
5 dried red chiles
1 bay leaf
4 green cardamom
1 cup broth or water
1 Tbs. garlic, minced
1 Tbs. ginger, minced
1 tsp. turmeric
4 Tbs. cooking oil
salt and pepper
2 Tbs. chopped cilantro for garnish

PREPARATION

In a large bowl, season chicken pieces with salt and pepper. Heat oil and brown chicken. Reserve brown chicken on a plate. Drain excess oil. In a non-stick saucepan, heat oil. To the hot oil, add whole red chiles and bay leaf; fry for 30 seconds. Add turmeric and chopped onion, and fry until brown. Put garlic and ginger into the onion mixture; fry for 30 seconds. To this mixture add cumin powder, curry powder, chili powder, bruised cardamom, salt and pepper. Mix well for a minute or so.

Transfer browned chicken pieces into the spice mixture; stir well. Add broth to the chicken mixture; set heat to low and let simmer until chicken pieces are tender and the sauce has thickened to a desired consistency, about 35-45 minutes. When cooked, turn off the heat and add chopped cilantro to garnish. Serve hot with rice and roti (flat bread).

FLEMING'S PRIME STEAKHOUSE & WINE BAR

1855 S. Lindbergh Blvd. 314-567-7610

BEEF FLEMINGTON

Ingredients
4 (6-oz.) filets
1 tsp. salt and pepper blend
2 Tbs. lightly salted butter
4 (5 x 5) puff pastry sheets
1 recipe of Mushroom Duxelle (see recipe)
2 pasteurized egg yolks
2 tsp. oil
1 cup Madeira Sauce
2 Tbs. parsley, chopped

PREPARATION

Cut the filet so the steak is 1-1/2 to 2 inches tall. Season the steak with salt and pepper and sear in a hot skillet with butter for 2-3 minutes each side until slightly brown. Let steaks cool. Cut puff pastry into 5 x 5-inch squares, then use a rolling pin to roll out to 6 x 6-inch squares. Spread Mushroom Duxelle evenly in the center of the puff pastry so that is about 1 inch from the sides. Set the filet on top, making sure the meat is dry. Pull the dough up around the sides of the filet, bringing the 4 points together in the center. (Do not overlap the dough.) Flip the steak over and lightly brush the dough with egg yolk. You can decorate the top of the steak with a piece of puff pastry.

To cook, place clarified butter on a hot metal sizzle plate, set beef on top and bake in a 400 degree oven to desired temperature. For medium rare, 12-14 minutes at 400 degrees. For medium, 15-16 minutes at 400 degrees. For medium well, 16-18 minutes at 350 degrees. (Baking times are approximate.) Place the Flemington on the plate and drizzle the Madeira Sauce around the plate. Garnish with chopped parsley.

Mushroom Duxelle Ingredients
1/4 lb. button mushrooms
1/4 lb. Portobello mushrooms, cleaned
1/4 lb. Shiitake mushrooms, stems removed
1/4 lb. butter, lightly salted, room temperature
1/2 Tbs. garlic, minced (see recipe)
1/4 cup brandy

Clean button mushrooms, remove stems and gills from portobellos, and remove stems from the shiitake. Cut all the mushrooms into 1/4-inch slices. In a large sauté pan, melt half the butter on high heat. Cook mushrooms for 4-5 minutes, add garlic and cook for 2-3 minutes more until golden brown. Add brandy and cook to reduce for 1 minute. When mushrooms are cool, place in a food processor and pulse to a fine mince. Add remaining butter and pulse to combine well.

SERVES 4

FRANK PAPA'S RISTORANTE

2241 South Brentwood Blvd. 314-961-3344

POLLO CON FUNGI

BAKED CHICKEN BREAST WITH A PORTOBELLO MUSHROOM
AND TOASTED PINE NUT STUFFING, TOPPED WITH SUN-
DRIED TOMATO BASIL PESTO CREAM SAUCE.

Ingredients and Preparation
4 pieces boneless chicken breast
Pound slightly, to be stuffed and rolled. Season with salt and pepper.

4 oz. clarified butter – large skillet, high heat
1/4 cup yellow onion, chopped - sauté
1 large portobello mushroom, chopped – sauté
1/2 cup white wine – add and reduce by half
1 cup breadcrumbs – add
1/2 cup chicken stock – add to bind
3 Tbs. roasted pine nuts – add and season with freshly ground pepper

SUN-DRIED TOMATO, BASIL, AND PESTO CREAM SAUCE

Ingredients and Preparation
3 oz. clarified butter – medium saucepan, high heat
4 Tbs. yellow onion, minced – sauté
1 tsp. garlic, minced – sauté
15 pcs. sun-dried tomato, chopped – sauté
2 Tbs. basil pesto – add
1/4 cup sherry wine – add, reduce by one-third
16 oz. heavy cream – add and reduce until it coats spoon
Season with white pepper and salt if needed

Stuff chicken breast, roll and skewer. Bake chicken in 9 x 13 baking dish, with small amount of chicken stock in bottom of dish (enough to make sure chicken breasts do not dry out). Cook at 400 degrees for 15-20 minutes. Slice crossways and serve on top of sauce.

FRANK PAPA'S RISTORANTE

2241 South Brentwood Blvd. 314-961-3344

VEAL MARSALA

Ingredients
3 oz. clarified butter
18 oz. scallopine veal
2 cups mushrooms, sliced
1 small bell pepper, julienne
1 small tomato, seedless, skinless, chopped
2 Tbs. garlic
1/2 cup Marsala wine
3 cups beef stock
4 Tbs. roux, 50 % butter, 50 % flour

PREPARATION

In hot skillet place 1 oz. of butter. Lightly flour veal and sauté. Continue adding butter and sauté veal until finished. In same skillet add remaining butter, mushrooms, green pepper and tomato. Cook for approximately 1 minute; add garlic. Pour in Marsala and reduce. Add beef stock and bring to a boil. Add your roux pats until sauce thickens. Reheat veal in oven, top with sauce and serve.

SINGAPORE BBQ PORK

Ingredients
Chinese BBQ Pork:
1 jar char siu marinade
3 lb. pork butt

For Sauté:
1/4 cup garlic, chopped
1/4 cup olive oil
1 cup onion, julienne
1 cup red pepper, julienne
1-1/2 lbs. cooked phad Thai noodles
bean sprouts
green onions

Sweet & Sour Sauce:
2 tsp. curry powder
1/2 cup sugar
1/3 cup soy sauce
1/2 cup ketchup
1/2 cup white vinegar
3/4 cup pineapple juice
1 Tbs. salt
1-1/2 cups chicken stock
3 Tbs. sriracha sauce

PREPARATION

Coat pork completely with char siu marinade and place in refrigerator for at least 2 hours (preferably overnight). Assemble all ingredients for sweet and sour sauce and whisk until all solids have dissolved. Roast pork in a 350-degree oven until internal temperature reaches 160 degrees (about an hour). After pork is cool, slice against the grain into thin strips and set aside. Slice all vegetables and prepare noodles. In a large sauté pan, heat oil and garlic. Add onions, red peppers, and approximately 2 cups of sliced pork; cook for 1 minute. Add sauce and stir well. Drain noodles very well. Add to pan and cook for 1 minute, stirring to incorporate sauce into noodles. Plate and garnish with bean sprouts and sliced green onion.

SERVES 4 WITH ENOUGH SAUCE AND PORK FOR 8 (JUST SAUTÉ TWICE)

GIANINO'S

3735 S. Lindbergh Blvd. 314-821-4140 www.gianinos.com

CHICKEN SPEDINI

Ingredients
24 oz. (1/2-inch thick) sliced chicken breast
4 oz. lemon juice
6 oz. olive oil
8 oz. Parmesan cheese
3 oz. parsley flakes
4 oz. garlic, chopped
2 cups breadcrumbs
4 cups Italian breadcrumbs
1 oz. coarse black pepper
2 Tbs. cracked red pepper
2 lbs. butter, melted
6 (10-inch) skewers
Lemons for garnish, cut into quarters

PREPARATION

Combine chicken, lemon juice, olive oil, Parmesan, parsley, garlic, black pepper, red pepper, and regular breadcrumbs. Combine in large bowl and marinate for 1 hour in refrigerator. Skewer chicken, dip into melted butter, and roll in Italian breadcrumbs. Cook on charbroil for 4 minutes on each side.

GIAN-TONY'S RISTORANTE

5356 Daggett Ave. 314-772-4893

INVOLTINI ALLA GIAN-TONY'S

Ingredients
eggplant
spinach
ricotta cheese
tomato sauce
Fontinella or mozzarella cheese
salt & black pepper

PREPARATION

Steam spinach and let cool to room temperature. Peel the skin off the eggplant and cut it lengthwise into very thin slices. Lightly sauté the slices in oil. Place the sautéed slices onto dry towels to drain excess oil, also cooling at room temperature.

Once the spinach is at room temperature, blend it with the ricotta cheese, 1/2 tsp. salt and 1/2 tsp. black pepper, until it is fine. Once the eggplant has reached room temperature, scoop approximately 2 oz. of the mix onto the eggplant and roll it. Top it with your tomato sauce and cheese and bake for approximately 15 minutes.

GIOVANNI'S

5201 Shaw Ave. 314-772-5598

PASTA PENETTE AL RADICCHIO

Ingredients
12 oz. penette
1/2 small head radicchio
2 cloves garlic
6 oz. 40% cream
2 oz. lightly salted butter
1 oz. Gorgonzola cheese
fresh Parmigiano, grated
1 tsp. extra virgin olive oil
2 oz. Burgundy wine

PREPARATION

Add olive oil and garlic to skillet and cook over medium flame until garlic caramelizes. When garlic is caramelized, add radicchio and half of butter. Continue to cook until radicchio is cooked, approximately 3 minutes. Add the wine, let reduce by half, and then add Gorgonzola cheese. Add cream and the rest of butter and let it reduce over medium flame. Put sauce to side.

Cook noodles in lightly salted water 5-7 minutes, to *al dente*. Strain pasta and add it to sauce; cook over high flame for one minute. Serve on a hot dinner plate, after topping with freshly grated Parmigiano cheese.

SERVES 4

GRAFFITI GLOBAL GRILL & BAR

HERB-BRAISED CHICKEN BREAST WITH WILD MUSHROOM JUS, GARLIC WILTED SPINACH AND DRIED TOMATOES

Herb Marinade Ingredients
1/4 cup fresh basil, chopped
1/4 cup fresh parsley, chopped
1/4 cup fresh rosemary, chopped
1/2 cup olive oil
2 Tbs. fresh garlic puree
1 Tbs. salt
1 tsp. black pepper

PREPARATION

Combine and mix all ingredients. Marinate chicken for at least 4 hours and up to 24 hours.

Garlic Spinach Ingredients
1 Tbs. olive oil
1 tsp. fresh garlic puree
2 oz. fresh spinach
salt and pepper to taste

Heat olive oil in a skillet over high heat for at least a minute. Remove from heat and add spinach and garlic while mixing to avoid overcooking. Season with salt and pepper.

Braised Chicken Ingredients
8 oz. boneless chicken breast
1 oz. herb marinade
2 oz. portobello mushrooms, sliced
2 oz. shiitake mushrooms, sliced
2 oz. white mushrooms, quartered
1/2 cup chicken stock
1 tsp. fresh garlic puree
1 Tbs. toasted pine nuts

Place a large skillet over medium high heat for one minute. When the skillet is hot, place the chicken skin side down and sear for about 4 minutes, until skin is crisp and golden brown. Turn chicken over and cook for another 2 minutes. Add chicken stock and garlic to skillet with the chicken and mushrooms and braise until chicken is cooked through, about 2 more minutes. Serve with wilted spinach and dried tomatoes.

GROWLER'S PUB

3811 S. Lindbergh 314-984-9009 www.growlerspub.com

SOUTHWESTERN QUESADILLA

Ingredients
2 flour tortillas
4 oz. blackened chicken
1/2 cup onion and pepper mix
1/2 cup smoked corn mixture
1/2 cup cheddar and Monterey jack cheese
1/2 cup pepper jack cheese
6 Tbs. Cajun seasoning
2 oz. salsa
1/4 cup shredded lettuce
2 Tbs. sour cream
1 Tbs. scallions, diced
2 Tbs. tomato, diced
4 Tbs. margarine
1 cup water
1 Tbs. Liquid Barbecue Smoke

Rub chicken breast with Cajun seasoning. Bake or grill until done. Let chicken cool, then dice. Mix onions, pepper and corn, and put into a perforated pan. In another pan mix water and Liquid Smoke. Insert perforated pan into this pan; cover tightly with foil. Bake in 350-degree oven for 20 minutes. Butter one side of flour tortilla and flip. Layer mixture of cheeses. Add chicken, onion-pepper mix, and corn. Heat in oven until chicken is hot and cheese is melted. Add other tortilla and butter and season and toast. Flip and toast other side. Cut into eight pieces. Serve on large oval platter and garnish with shredded lettuce, sour cream, scallions, diced tomatoes, and salsa.

HACIENDA MEXICAN RESTAURANT

9748 Manchester Rd. 314-962-7100 www.hacienda-stl.com

MOLE DE GALLINA
(MOH-LEH DEH GAH –YEE-NAH)

Ingredients
4 oz. chicken mole paste
1-1/4 qts. hot water
2 bay leaves
1-1/4 oz. chicken base
1/4 tsp. oregano
1 tsp. garlic powder
1/4 cup peanuts, finely chopped
1/4 cup brown sugar
1 tsp. onion powder
1 lb. chicken strips or tenders, washed, drained and patted dry
Seasoning for coating chicken
1/2 cup flour
1 tsp. garlic powder
1 tsp. black pepper
1 tsp. salt

Dissolve mole paste in hot water. Add the next seven ingredients and simmer for approximately 15 minutes. Lightly dust chicken strips in seasoned flour and sauté for 5 minutes. Add chicken to the sauce and simmer until chicken is tender. May be made ahead and reheated just before serving. Serving suggestions: make Spanish rice and serve as a bed or on the side. Wrap in warm flour tortillas.

SERVES 4

HARPO'S CHESTERFIELD

136 Hilltown Village 636-537-1970

CHICKEN CHOP-OTULA

Ingredients
2 (6-oz.) chicken breasts
2 large potatoes
1/3-1/4 sliced smoked ham
2 cups mushrooms, sliced or quartered
6 green onions
blackening spice (see recipe)
Tasso Hollandaise sauce (see recipe)
extra virgin olive oil

Blackening Spice Ingredients
2 Tbs. paprika
1/2 tsp. cayenne
1/2 tsp garlic
1/2 tsp. onion powder
1/4 tsp. white pepper
1/4 tsp. black pepper
1 tsp. thyme leaves
1 tsp. oregano leaves
1 Tbs. salt
1 Tbs. sugar
mix thoroughly

Tasso Hollandaise Sauce Ingredients
1/4 cup butter
2 egg yolks, beaten
1/4 cup half and half
1 tsp. lemon juice
1/2 tsp. dry mustard
1/4 tsp. salt
1/2 cup ham, diced

PREPARATION

Melt butter over low heat. Mix in yolks, cream, lemon juice, dry mustard, and salt over medium heat for 1 to 1-1/2 minutes or until the mixture begins to thicken; then remove from heat. Add ham and blackening spice to your liking. Take uncooked potatoes and make four cuts lengthwise on each. Then dice into evenly cubed sections. Place cubed potatoes on an oiled sheet pan and bake at 350 degrees for 7-9 minutes or until golden brown.

Cook chicken breasts while potatoes are cooking. Put 1/4 cup of extra virgin olive oil into a hot skillet. Add potatoes, mushrooms, green onions, salt and pepper, mixing constantly. Remove from flame when mushrooms are fully sautéed. Drain any excess oil and portion on plate. Place chicken breast on top and drizzle Tasso Hollandaise Sauce over the top. Garnish with green onions and serve.

SERVES 2

INDIA'S RASOI

7923 Forsyth Blvd. 314-727-1414 www.rasoi.com
4569 Laclede Ave. 314-361-6911 www.rasoi.com

TANDOORI CHICKEN

A tandoor is an earthen oven that is sort of cylindrical and uses charcoal to cook the meat or bread. This recipe will need a barbecue grill as a substitute. It can also be cooked in a gas or electric oven, but it will lose most of the flavor. Also, the chicken has to be marinated for at least 6 hours, ideally 12 hours overnight.

Ingredients
12 chicken drumsticks and/or breast pieces, skin removed
1 cup plain yogurt or 2 cups buttermilk
1-1/2 Tbs. red chili powder
2 Tbs. coriander powder
1 Tbs. garlic powder, freshly ground
1 Tbs. ginger powder, freshly ground
1 Tbs. cumin powder
1/2 Tbs. garam masala powder
2 Tbs. salt
onion

PREPARATION

For the marinade, add the yogurt plus 1 cup of water, or the buttermilk with no water, into the bowl. Add all the spices from 3 thru 7 into the bowl and stir to form a mixture. Add chicken pieces into the mixture so they are all covered with the paste/mixture. Cover the bowl with a lid and let it stand for 6 hours. If you plan to marinate for 12-15 hours, put it in the refrigerator. The more time it is marinated, the better it will absorb the spices and the tastier it will be.

When grilling chicken, apply melted butter to the chicken pieces with a brush or spoon all over and grill on the barbecue in the normal fashion. Turn over the chicken pieces when they look brownish red in color or darker if you prefer it well done. Slice the onion into rings; add some salt and lemon juice to it, to be served as a salad with the tandoori chicken. Lemon juice squeezed on the cooked pieces also adds to the flavor.

SERVES 4

JAVA TENDERLOIN

Maple Chipotle Sauce Ingredients
2 Tbs. olive oil
4 cloves garlic, peeled and minced
1 shallot, peeled and minced
1/2 chipotle pepper in adobo sauce (Mexican seasoning paste of ground chiles, herbs, vinegar)
1/8 cup bourbon
2-1/2 cups veal stock (homemade or prepared)
1/4 cup maple syrup
salt and pepper to taste
1 tsp. arrowroot

Gorgonzola Caramelized Onions Ingredients
2 Tbs. olive oil
2 medium onions, peeled and julienne
2 oz. Gorgonzola cheese
salt and pepper to taste

Beef Tenderloin Ingredients
4 (6-oz.) center-cut beef tenderloin
salt and pepper to taste
1/2 cup Amaretto coffee made with freshly ground beans

Garnish
Mashed potatoes

PREPARATION

In a hot skillet with olive oil, sauté garlic, shallot, and chipotle pepper for about 2 minutes. Deglaze pan with bourbon. Add veal stock, maple syrup, salt and pepper. Let reduce by half. Add arrowroot and strain sauce through fine sieve; keep warm.

In a skillet with olive oil, sauté onion until the sugars release and the onions become a nice deep caramel color. Add cheese and season with salt and pepper.

Season beef with salt and pepper. Touch each cut side of beef in the Amaretto coffee. Roast in 350-degree oven to desired doneness. Slice tenderloin on a bias. Arrange meat around mashed potatoes. Top potatoes with onion; drizzle sauce over tenderloin.

SERVES 4

JIMMY'S CAFÉ ON THE PARK

706 DeMun Ave. 314-725-8585 www.jimmyscafe.com

OATMEAL-CRUSTED CHICKEN

Sauce Ingredients
1 clove garlic, peeled and minced
1 shallot, peeled and minced
1 Tbs. olive oil
1/2 cup mushrooms, sliced
1 Tbs. chicken base or bouillon granules
1/4 cup dry white wine
2 cups heavy cream
grated zest and juice of 1/2 lemon
grated zest and juice of 1/2 lime
3 or 4 fresh sage leaves
salt
ground black pepper

Chicken
2 eggs
1 cup rolled oats
1/4 cup all purpose flour
1/4 cup cornmeal
1 Tbs. garlic powder
2 Tbs. dried Italian seasoning
1/2 tsp. ground red cayenne pepper
1 Tbs. marjoram
1 Tbs. sweet paprika
3/4 tsp. salt
3/4 tsp. ground black pepper
8 boneless skinless chicken breast halves
1/2 cup olive oil
diced fresh tomatoes for garnish

PREPARATION

For the sauce, sauté garlic and shallot in olive oil for 2 minutes. Add mushrooms and sauté 2 to 3 minutes more. Stir in chicken base and white wine. Simmer, uncovered, until liquid is reduced by half. Stir in cream, citrus zests and citrus juices. Cook, stirring, until sauce is smooth and thickens slightly. Do not let sauce boil.

Add sage, salt and pepper to taste. Sauce will be thin. (Sauce can be made ahead.) Let cool completely, then refrigerate. Reheat slowly over low heat.

To prepare the chicken, preheat oven to 350 degrees. Beat eggs. In a separate bowl, combine oats, flour, cornmeal, garlic powder, Italian seasoning, red pepper, marjoram, paprika, salt and pepper. Dip chicken in beaten eggs, and then coat with oatmeal mixture. Heat oil in an ovenproof skillet over medium high heat. Sauté chicken in oil until lightly browned on both sides. Transfer to oven. Bake until chicken is done in center, about 10 minutes.

Pour sauce over chicken. Garnish with diced fresh tomatoes. This chicken has an excellent crispy, Southwestern crust that goes well with the mild, creamy sauce. A good recipe to make ahead, cooking the chicken just before serving.

SERVES 4

JOANIE'S PIZZERIA

2101 Menard St. 314-865-1994 www.joanies.com

BLACKENED CHICKEN PENNE

Ingredients
4 (6-oz.) boneless chicken breasts
1 lb. penne noodles (cooked)
1 cup chicken stock
1/2 cup white wine
2 cups mushrooms, sliced
2 cups tomatoes, diced
1 cup red onion, sliced
2 Tbs. garlic, minced
1/2 cup Cajun blackening spice (see below)
3 Tbs. olive oil
1/4 cup Parmesan cheese, shredded

Cajun Blackening Spice Ingredients
5 Tbs. paprika
1 Tbs. cayenne powder
1 Tbs. onion powder
1 Tbs. garlic powder
2 tsp. salt
1 tsp. white pepper, ground
1 tsp. dried thyme, crushed
1 tsp. dried oregano, crushed

PREPARATION

Season chicken breasts with Cajun blackening spice. Grill seasoned breast while preparing pasta. In large skillet, sauté red onion, mushrooms and garlic until tender. Add chicken stock, white wine and 2 Tbs. blackening spice. Bring to boil. Add cooked penne noodles and diced tomatoes. Toss and cook until thickened.

Arrange pasta on serving dish; top with grilled chicken breast. Garnish with freshly shredded Parmesan cheese.

SERVES 4

JOHN D. McGURK'S IRISH PUB

1200 Russell Blvd. 314-776-8309

LAMB STEW

Ingredients
5 lbs. lamb, cut from fresh lamb leg
1 qt. russet potatoes, diced into 1-inch cubes
2 cups carrots, diced 3/4 inch
1 cup celery, diced
1 cup onions, diced
2 Tbs. celery salt
3 Tbs. garlic, chopped
1 gal. lamb or beef stock
2 Tbs. dry leaf thyme
1 bay leaf
olive oil

Brown the meat in small amount of olive oil. Add garlic, seasoning and vegetables. Stir to coat vegetables and add stock. Simmer until meat is tender. Stir in slurry of flour and water (equal parts of each) until moderately thick and stew like. Simmer for a short time longer and add salt, pepper, and seasoning for taste. Serve with Irish soda bread.

JOHNNY GITTO'S

6997 Chippewa St. 314-781-8111

PRIMAVERA PASTA

Ingredients
1 zucchini, cut into nickel-size pieces
1 tomato, cut into bite-sized pieces
3 stalks fresh broccoli, cut into bite-sized pieces
1 carrot, cut into 2-inch sticks
1 oz. fresh mushrooms, cut
12 pieces baby corn
1 lb. of your favorite pasta, cooked
3 Tbs. olive oil
1 tsp. cornstarch
4 cloves of garlic, minced
6 oz. chicken bouillon
red pepper flakes, fresh basil, salt and pepper

Put oil and garlic into a hot skillet or wok. Get it very hot, then add vegetables, leaving the tomatoes for last. Stirring briskly so as not to burn, but brown, add the following spices to taste: salt & pepper, red pepper flakes, and fresh chopped sweet basil. Let cook, stirring, for about 5 minutes; then add chicken bouillon and the tomatoes. Dissolve cornstarch in cold water and add to ingredients. (The cornstarch is to give the dish a shiny appearance while marrying all of the ingredients.) Fold the pasta into the mixture. Plate on a large platter, sprinkle with Parmesan cheese, and serve immediately.

Note: I make this dish with chicken breasts and shrimp. I use 2 (4-oz.) breasts, and about 6 (26 count) shrimp. When I use the above, I add red wine to the sauté, and I mix a little of the seasoned breadcrumbs into the Parmesan cheese. Progresso breadcrumbs are as good as making them yourself.

JW'S OFF THE PARK

GONE BUT NOT FORGOTTEN

BOURBON SHRIMP

Ingredients
3 Tbs. butter
1/4 tsp. salt
1/8 tsp. thyme
1/8 tsp. fine black pepper
1/2 Tbs. garlic, minced
1 lb. (20-26 count) shrimp, peeled and deveined
1/4 cup bourbon
1/4 cup heavy cream

PREPARATION

Melt butter in skillet and add spices. Add shrimp and sauté until pink. Splash shrimp with bourbon and
remove to serving dish and keep warm.

Add cream to skillet, scraping bottom of pan with spoon as you mix in the cream. Heat mixture over
medium heat and pour over shrimp. Garnish plate. Serve immediately.

KEY WEST CAFÉ

1820 Market St. 314-241-2566

BBQ SHRIMP

Ingredients
1 cup garlic, minced fine
50 whole bay leaves, crushed
1/2 cup crushed rosemary
1/4 cup oregano
1/4 cup salt
1/2 cup paprika
1/2 cup Liquid Smoke
1/3 cup black pepper
1/4 cup red pepper
2 cups chili sauce
6 lbs. butter
6 qt. vegetable oil
2 Tbs. Tabasco sauce
1 cup Worcestershire sauce
shrimp

PREPARATION

Combine ingredients over heat until mixed. Store in 5-gallon pot. To cook shrimp, sauté with 6-oz.
ladle of sauce for 2 minutes.

KINGSPOINT

7645 Magna Dr., Belleville, IL 618-277-7715

CARLI'S ROTINI PESTO

Ingredients
8 oz. cooked rotini (skroodle) noodles
6 oz. heavy cream
2 Tbs. sun-dried tomatoes, julienne
1 Tbs. pesto (see below)
2 tsp. Parmesan cheese
salt and pepper to taste
chopped parsley or basil

Pesto:
1/4 lb. fresh basil
2 oz. olive oil
5 whole garlic cloves, peeled
1/4 cup toasted pine nuts
1/2 cup grated Parmesan

PREPARATION

Blend all pesto ingredients until smooth.

Place heavy cream in sauté pan and begin to heat slowly. When cream reaches a boil, add sun-dried tomatoes and pesto; wait 2 minutes and add noodles. Cook another two minutes and add Parmesan. Season as necessary with salt and pepper, then remove from heat. Toss all together and place in serving bowl. Garnish with Parmesan and chopped parsley or basil.

LLYWELYN'S

4747 McPherson Ave. 314-361-3003 www.llywelynspub.com

WELSH ONION AND POTATO PIE

Ingredients
Puff pastry squares
10 large potatoes, parboiled and sliced thin
4 large onions, sliced thin
4 red bell peppers, diced
1 lb. white cheddar, shredded
2 tsp. sage
1 tsp. black pepper
1 lb. snap peas, cut in half
1 cup Welsh whiskey or ale
1 lb. butter
1/4 cup granulated garlic
1-1/2 Tbs. chicken base

PREPARATION

Cook all ingredients in butter until tender. Spoon 4 oz. of the mixture into each puff pastry square. Fold over, cinch edges together. Bake in 350-degree oven until golden brown.

LORENZO'S TRATTORIA

1933 Edwards St. 314-773-2223

RIGATONI

Ingredients
1 lb. cooked rigatoni noodles
2 cups basic tomato sauce
1 cup white wine
4 cloves garlic, minced
1 small eggplant, diced
1/4 cup capers
1/3 cup kalamata olives
3 fresh mozzarella balls, diced
3 sprigs fresh basil, julienne
1/3 cup olive oil
salt and pepper to taste

PREPARATION

Sauté eggplant in olive oil until it is golden brown. Add garlic, capers and kalamata olive and sauté for 30 seconds. Next add white wine and reduce by half. Add tomato sauce and basil. Season with salt and pepper. Add mozzarella and pasta to eggplant mixture, toss and serve.

SERVES 6

LORUSSO'S CUCINA

3122 Watson Rd. 314-647-6222 www.lorussos.com

BISTECCA MUDEGA

Ingredients
1-1/2 lb. tenderloin medallions or your favorite meat
1-1/2 Tbs. olive oil
1 Tbs. sherry
1 Tbs. Italian breadcrumbs
1 Tbs. Parmesan cheese
1 tsp. garlic
6 turns of pepper mill

For the sauce:
1 cup Limone Sauce (see recipe)
1 Tbs. garlic, chopped
1/2 cup mushrooms, sliced
2 oz. prosciutto
2 oz. provel

PREPARATION

Marinate meat, oil, sherry, Parmesan, garlic, and pepper for at least 6 hours. Roll in Italian breadcrumbs and broil to desired doneness. Heat all sauce items except provel cheese. Top the meat with cheese, then sauce.

LIMONE SAUCE

Ingredients
3/4 cup water
1/8 cup white wine
1 tsp. butter
1 tsp. lemon juice
1/2 Tbs. half and half
1 tsp. chicken base
1/2 tsp. cornstarch
1 Tbs. water

Combine all ingredients except starch and water. Heat until low boil. Combine starch and water. Add slowly while stirring. Keeps 6 days in refrigerator.

MAKES 1 CUP

LORUSSO'S CUCINA

3122 Watson Rd. 314-647-6222 www.lorussos.com

CIOPPINO

Ingredients
2 cups Mussel Sauce (see recipe)
2 caps saffron
2 oz. white wine
1 (5-oz.) lobster tail, split
4 oz. scallops
3 oz. shrimp
4 oz. swordfish or other firm fish
4 fresh clams
8 fresh mussels
1/4 cup cooked rice or pasta

PREPARATION

Combine all ingredients. Cook, covered, at medium high heat for 10 minutes or until lobster is cooked through. Serve with garlic toast.

SERVES 2 DINNERS OR 4 APPETIZERS

MUSSEL SAUCE

Ingredients
2 cups prepared marinara sauce
1 cup Limone Sauce (see recipe p. 72)
1/2 Tbs. white wine
2 Tbs. fresh basil, chopped
pinch red pepper
pinch cracked black pepper
pinch salt
1 Tbs. garlic, chopped

Combine all items and chill. Keeps for 5 days in the refrigerator. This sauce is used for mussels and Cioppino. Also makes a great pasta sauce!

SERVES 4

LUCAS PARK GRILLE

1234 Washington Ave. 314-241-7770

STRUDEL

Ingredients
1 pkg. phyllo dough
6 oz. black trumpet mushrooms (or other wild mushrooms of choice)
6 oz. braised lamb shank
3 pears, cored and cut into large dices
3 Tbs. apple cider vinegar
2 Tbs. brown sugar
2 Tbs. melted butter
2 oz. Madeira

PREPARATION

Whisk brown sugar and vinegar until smooth. Toss pears in vinegar/brown sugar mixture to coat. Lay flat on a sheet tray. Roast in 375-degree oven until soft, approximately 18-20 minutes. Clean and slice the mushrooms. Sauté until liquid is gone. Deglaze with Madeira. Toss lamb, mushrooms and pears together in a bowl. Brush first layer of phyllo with melted butter. Add large spoonful of mixture across and roll. Brush next layer and roll again. Repeat for four layers. Bake in 375-degree oven until brown, approximately 10 minutes.

SERVES 4

LYNCH STREET BISTRO

GONE BUT NOT FORGOTTEN

PAN-SEARED SESAME SALMON WITH CHILLED SOBA NOODLE SALAD

Ingredients
2 (8-oz.) salmon fillets, boneless, skinless
1/2 cup sesame seeds
2 cups soba noodles, cooked al dente
1/2 cup red onions, julienne
1/2 cup zucchini, julienne
1/2 cup carrots, julienne
1/2 cup red bell peppers, julienne
1 cup chili garlic sauce
2 Tbs. olive oil

PREPARATION

Toss soba noodles, julienne vegetables and chili garlic sauce and set aside for later. Completely coat the salmon fillet in sesame seeds. Heat olive oil in a skillet until hot but not smoking. Place salmon in skillet and cook until sesame seeds start to brown and then flip the fillets. Place skillet in oven and cook the salmon to proper temperature. Drain excess sauce from the noodle salad. Mound the noodle salad in the center of the plate and top with the salmon. Top off with a little Chili Garlic Sauce or a spicy Thai pepper sauce.

SERVES 2

CHILI GARLIC SAUCE

Ingredients
1-1/2 cups soy sauce
1/2 cup hoisin sauce
1 cup sweet pepper sauce
1/2 cup rice wine vinegar
1 cup mirin

Blend all ingredients and refrigerate until needed.

SERVES 9

LYNCH STREET BISTRO

GONE BUT NOT FORGOTTEN

SWEET HORSERADISH AND GRAIN MUSTARD GLAZED PORK PORTERHOUSE

Ingredients
2 (14-oz.) pork porterhouse
1/2 lb. butter
1 cup brown sugar
3 Tbs. stone ground mustard
3 Tbs. prepared horseradish

PREPARATION

Melt butter in a medium pot. Add brown sugar, stir until thickened, then add mustard and horseradish.

Grill pork over open flame, basting occasionally with glaze until desired temperature is reached. Suggested temperature is medium rare to medium.

McMURPHY'S

614 N. 11th St. 314-231-3006

IRISH STEW

Ingredients
5 lbs. stew meat
3 yellow onions, medium diced
3 large carrots, medium diced
1 stalk celery, medium diced
2 lbs. turnips, medium diced
2 lbs. potatoes, peeled and diced
2 gallons water
1/4 lb. minor beef base
1 Tbs. thyme
1 Tbs. oregano
1 Tbs. basil
1 tsp. salt
1 tsp. black pepper
1-1/2 lbs. butter
16 oz. flour

PREPARATION

Peel and dice all vegetables. Brown stew meat with 1/2 pound butter. Add ALL ingredients into large pot with beef base and water on high heat. In a separate pot, melt 1 pound butter, then add flour to make a roux. Add roux to stock. Reduce to medium heat for 15 minutes. Cook for 1 hour, and then serve.

MORTON'S OF CHICAGO

7822 Bonhomme Ave. 314-725-4008 www.mortons.com

BROILED SEA SCALLOPS WRAPPED IN BACON, APRICOT CHUTNEY

Ingredients
12 large (1-1.5 oz.) sea scallops
12 slices bacon
8 spinach leaves, washed, and stems removed
2 Tbs. melted butter
1/2 cup Apricot Chutney (see recipe)
2 lemons, halved
4 bamboo skewers

PREPARATION

Place bacon strips on a wire rack in a 350-degree oven. Cook until half done, approximately 13 minutes. Remove bacon from oven and wrap each scallop with a bacon strip. Slide three bacon-wrapped scallops on each bamboo skewer, leaving a 1-inch gap between scallops. Place skewered scallops in buttered pie tin. Brush scallops lightly with melted butter. Place in broiler for 8 minutes, turning once after 4 minutes.

To serve, place two spinach leaves in center of each plate. Place one ounce of apricot chutney on one spinach leaf of each plate. Place lemon half on each plate. Remove scallops from broiler. Remove bamboo skewer and arrange three scallops on top of the other spinach leaf. Serve immediately.

Apricot Chutney Ingredients
1 cup Smucker's apricot marmalade
1/2 cup prepared horseradish, strained
2 tsp. freshly cracked black pepper

In stainless steel bowl, smooth marmalade with whip. Add horseradish and cracked pepper. Blend thoroughly and refrigerate. Chutney can be kept refrigerated up to 3 weeks.

YIELDS 8 OZ.

NEW ORLEANS BY-YOU
CRAB SHACK RESTAURANT

GONE BUT NOT FORGOTTEN

SEAFOOD CREOLE

Ingredients
1 lb. shrimp, crawfish, crabmeat, or fish
1/4 cup vegetable oil
1-1/2 cups hot water
1/4 cup flour
1 (8-oz.) can tomato sauce
1 (16-oz.) can diced tomatoes
1/2 cup onions, chopped
1/2 cup chopped parsley
1/4 cup green peppers, chopped
4 garlic cloves, finely chopped
1/4 cup butter
1 tsp. cayenne pepper (substitute white pepper for added spice)
1/2 tsp. lemon juice
1/2 tsp. thyme
1 tsp. Cajun seasoning

PREPARATION

Prepare a roux by heating oil in a large skillet over a medium heat, gradually blending in flour with a whisk. Stir constantly until brown and smooth in texture. (Be careful not to scorch.) Gradually add water and stir until thick and creamy. Sauté onions, green pepper, and garlic in butter until soft; then add to roux and stir. Add remaining ingredients.
Simmer for 15 minutes. Serve over hot white rice.

MAKES APPROXIMATELY 6 SERVINGS

CRAWFISH ETTOUFFÉE

Ingredients
1/2 lb. butter
3/4 cup flour
1/4 cup green onions, chopped
1/4 cup green bell pepper
1/4 cup red bell pepper
1/2 cup celery, chopped
2 lbs. crawfish, tail meat with fat if possible
2 cloves garlic, minced
1 cup onion, chopped fine
1/2 cup fresh parsley
1 tsp. salt
Creole seasoning or black and red pepper to taste
Tabasco to taste
dash lemon juice
1/2 cup white wine
chicken stock or broth

PREPARATION

Melt butter and flour in a large saucepan over medium heat to form golden brown roux. Next add onions, celery, garlic and bell peppers. Sweat in roux until soft, about 20 minutes. Add red and black peppers, salt, Tabasco, lemon juice and wine. Slowly add broth to form creamy consistency.

Stir in crawfish and cook for an additional 15 minutes, adding broth as needed. Sprinkle in parsley and cook for 5 more minutes. Top with green onions and serve over rice. Garnish with cooked crawfish. Serve with crusty French bread and your favorite white wine.

NORTON'S CAFÉ

808 Geyer St. 314-436-0828

BLACKENED CATFISH

Ingredients
1 (7-9 oz.) catfish fillet
Norton's Café blackened seasoning**
2-3 Tbs. vegetable oil

PREPARATION

Dredge catfish fillet in Norton's blackened seasoning and shake off excess. Heat oil in skillet until almost smoking (approximately 300 degrees). Place fillet in oil and allow to cook for 7 to 8 minutes (do not burn). Turn fillet and repeat. Remove fillet and serve.

Suggested side dishes: sautéed vegetables, white or dirty rice, jambalaya or corn fritters. Substitutions: other fish fillets may be used. Cooking times will vary.

SERVES 1

** Norton's Café blackened seasoning available at Nortons Café & Dierbergs Markets.

THE PASTA HOUSE CO.

1143 Macklind Ave. 314-535-6644

FETTUCCINE ALFREDO

Ingredients
10 oz. cooked fettuccine noodles
8 oz. cream (half and half)
1 oz. butter
1/4 cup grated Parmigiano cheese

PREPARATION

Cook noodles in salted water until 3/4 done. Strain off water and put noodles back in pot. Add cream and butter. Bring to a hard boil. When noodles are fully cooked, remove from heat. Add Parmigiano cheese and cracked black pepper. Toss and serve.

SERVES 1-2

PATTY LONG CATERING, INC.
9TH STREET ABBEY

112 Sidney Street 314-776-0989

GRILLED PORK TENDERLOIN WITH A MOROCCAN BARBECUE SAUCE

Moroccan Barbecue Sauce Ingredients
1 cup honey
1 cup maple syrup
1/2 cup soy sauce
1 cup bottled barbecue sauce (preferably Maull's Original)
2 oz. lemon juice
1 tsp. garlic powder
1 tsp. white pepper
1 pinch cinnamon
1 pinch ginger

PREPARATION

Combine all ingredients, bring to a boil, season to taste and thicken slightly with a slurry of cornstarch.

Pork Marinade Ingredients
1 cup olive oil
1/2 cup soy sauce
1/8 cup lemon juice
1/4 cup rice wine vinegar
1 cup brown sugar
1 Tbs. red pepper
1 Tbs. garlic powder
1/4 cup kosher salt
1 Tbs. white pepper
1 Tbs. onion powder
2 Tbs. thyme
1 Tbs. cinnamon
1 Tbs. ginger

Combine all ingredients and marinate pork for at least 2 hours or overnight. Grill on a charcoal fire with additional hickory chips soaked in beer. Serve hot or cold with the barbecue sauce.

PAUL'S IN CLAYTON

GONE BUT NOT FORGOTTEN

FARFALLE WITH LOBSTER

Ingredients
2 lbs. farfalle pasta (bow ties)
1 qt. half and half
4 oz. fresh mushrooms, sliced
4 oz. marinara sauce
12 oz. fresh lobster meat, diced
2 oz. dry sherry
4 oz. grated Parmesan cheese
2 Tbs. parsley, chopped
salt and pepper to taste

PREPARATION

Cook the pasta according to package directions and set aside. In a large saucepan, pour in the cream and allow to reduce by 1/4 of original volume. Add mushrooms, lobster, and sherry wine. Boil for 3-5 minutes. Stir in grated Parmesan cheese and marinara sauce. Toss farfalle into the sauce and season with salt and pepper to taste. Serve hot.

SERVES 4

PINE POINT

GONE BUT NOT FORGOTTEN

PINE POINT MEATLOAF

Ingredients
1 lb. ground beef
1 lb. coarse-ground country pork sausage
4 oz. Italian breadcrumbs
1 tsp. oregano
8 strips thick-cut smoked bacon
1 egg

Pine Point Meatloaf Glace
6 oz. southern-style BBQ sauce
6 oz. ketchup

PREPARATION

By hand, mix together beef and pork until thoroughly combined. Add the egg and oregano. Gradually add the breadcrumbs to the mixture and continue to mix until all ingredients are combined. Form mixture into loaf. Lay bacon over the top of the loaf (perpendicular) and tuck underneath. Bake in 375-degree oven for 25-35 minutes. Slice and drizzle with Meatloaf Glace.

SERVES 4-6

PORTABELLA

15 N. Central Ave. 314-725-6588

PORTOBELLO MUSHROOM CANNELLONI

Ingredients
1 Tbs. olive oil
1/2 medium onion
1 tsp. garlic, chopped
1/4 lb. shiitake mushrooms, stems removed
1/4 lb. button mushrooms
1/4 lb. portobello mushrooms (can use stems)
1 roma tomato
1/2 cup ricotta cheese
1 oz. Asiago cheese
2 Tbs. basil, chopped
1 oz. spinach, chopped
12 won ton skins
1 beaten egg

PREPARATION

Heat olive oil in a large sauté pan until hot. Add shallots and garlic and sweat for 45 seconds. Add mushrooms and tomatoes, stirring occasionally. Let cook until mushrooms are dry. Add spinach and cook into mixture. Remove from the pan and let cool on a sheet tray. Once mix is cooled, fold in ricotta and Asiago cheeses. Blanch won ton skins in boiling water for 8 seconds and then shock in cold water bath. Place won ton skins on a damp towel that is sprinkled with Asiago cheese. Pipe mushroom mixture at bottom of each skin, paint egg wash at top of each skin, and roll mixture tight inside of each skin.

PORCINI CRUSTED SEA BASS

WITH ASPARAGUS, OVEN DRIED TOMATOES, ROASTED SHALLOTS IN A MUSHROOM BROTH

Mushroom Broth Ingredients

1 shallot, chopped
1 clove garlic, chopped
3 oz. celery, chopped
3 oz. carrot, chopped
3 oz. onion, chopped
3 stems thyme
1 lb. mushroom stems and scraps
3 qts. water or chicken stock
kosher salt to taste
2 Tbs. olive oil
1/4 cup dry porcini mushrooms

PREPARATION

In a hot pot with olive oil, sweat garlic and shallot. Add celery, carrot and onion and cook until onion is transparent. Add mushroom stem and scraps and sweat for 5-7 minutes. Add water or chicken stock and salt and let simmer for 30-45 minutes or until it has a rich mushroom flavor.

Roasted Shallot Ingredients

6-8 shallots, peeled
3 Tbs. olive oil
1 pinch kosher salt

Heat olive oil in a sauté pan at medium heat. Add the whole peeled shallots with salt and sauté until shallots are coated well with olive oil, about 2-3 minutes. Place in a 425-degree oven and roast for 15-20 minutes or until soft. Remove from sauté pan to a sheet pan and let cool. When cooled, remove outer skin and discard.

Oven-Dried Tomatoes Ingredients

9 roma tomatoes
2 oz. olive oil
1 pinch kosher salt
1 pinch black pepper

Remove core from tomatoes and then cut in half lengthwise. Place in a mixing bowl and toss with olive oil, salt and pepper. Place on a sheet tray and put in a preheated 200-degree oven and let cook for 6-8 hours. Remove and let cool.

Sea Bass Ingredients

6 (6-oz.) pcs. sea bass, red snapper, halibut, turbot or any flavorful white fish
3 Tbs. olive oil
1 cup porcini powder
1 Tbs. each salt and pepper

Season fish with salt and pepper and dust on flesh side with porcini powder. In a large sauté pan, add olive oil and wait until very hot. Place fish in pan, skin side up. Let cook for about 2 minutes and then place in oven. Depending on thickness, cook fish 2-3 minutes and flip in oven. Continue cooking for 2-3 more minutes and remove from oven. Use shallots, oven dried tomatoes and asparagus for garnish around fish and ladle about 1 oz. of mushroom broth per serving. Note: This remains a restaurant favorite since one of our very first menus!

RIGAZZI'S

4945 Daggett Ave. 314-772-4900

ZITI PASTA POMIDORO

Ingredients
1-1/2 cups (3 sticks) unsalted butter or margarine
1 clove garlic, minced
1/2 lb. fresh mushrooms, sliced
1 Tbs. salt, divided
1 tsp. black pepper
1 bunch broccoli, cut into florets (about 5 cups)
2 medium tomatoes, cut into 1-inch cubes (about 1-1/2 cups)
1/2 cup sliced black olives
2 qts. water
1 Tbs. vegetable oil or olive oil
1 lb. ziti or other pasta, uncooked
1/2 cup grated Parmesan cheese
3, 4-oz. cooked boneless, skinless chicken breast cut into strips (or)
12 jumbo cooked, peeled, deveined shrimp if desired

PREPARATION

Melt butter in 2-qt. saucepan. Add garlic, mushrooms, 1/2 Tbs. salt and pepper. Sauté over medium heat 5-8 minutes, or until mushrooms are softened. Stir in broccoli. Reduce heat slightly. Cook, uncovered, 10-12 minutes, or until broccoli is tender but crisp. (Do not overcook.) Add tomatoes and olives. Simmer 10 minutes, or until tomatoes and broccoli are tender. Cover and keep warm over very low heat. This makes about 5-1/2 cups of sauce.

Meanwhile, bring water, oil and the remaining salt to a boil in large saucepan. Add pasta; cook 8-10 minutes, or until done. Drain. In large mixing bowl, toss drained pasta, sauce and Parmesan cheese until well mixed. Place the mixture on a large serving platter. Top with chicken or shrimp, and additional Parmesan cheese, if desired.

YIELDS 12 CUPS, ABOUT 6 SERVINGS

RIZZO'S

(Debbir Rizzo, location by Ted Drewes, this location now closed)

CHICKEN SPEIDINI

Ingredients
7 (8 oz.) boneless, skinless chicken breasts
lemon juice
olive oil
pinch red pepper flakes
1 tsp. fresh garlic, chopped
Italian seasoned breadcrumbs
1 Tbs. Parmesan cheese (optional)
melted butter or margarine (optional)

PREPARATION

Cut chicken breasts into pieces a little larger than bite sized. Mix olive oil, juice of one lemon, garlic, and red pepper flakes. Coat chicken in mixture and marinate for 1 hour. Lightly coat in the breadcrumbs and Parmesan. Skewer chicken and char broil. Serve with melted butter or margarine and lemon wedges.

RUBY'S BRENTWOOD INN

GONE BUT NOT FORGOTTEN

CHICKEN DIANE

Ingredients
1 tsp. olive oil
4 skinless chicken breasts
2 green onions, chopped
1/2 cup fresh parsley, chopped
1/2 cup chicken base
1 Tbs. sherry
1-1/2 tsp. cornstarch
1 tsp. Dijon mustard
1/2 tsp. salt
1/2 tsp. margarine
1 Tbs. lemon juice

PREPARATION

In a large non-stick skillet, heat oil over medium heat. Add chicken; cook until browned. Turn and cook until all pink is gone.

In a blender or food processor, process green onions, parsley, broth, sherry, cornstarch, mustard and salt, until smooth.

Transfer chicken to serving platter. Add margarine and broth mixture to skillet. Cook until slightly thickened (about two minutes). Remove from heat; stir in lemon juice. Spoon sauce over the chicken. Serve.

MOROCCAN STYLE LAMB

Ingredients
4 onions, diced
5 lbs. leg of lamb, trimmed and cubed
1/2 cup garlic, minced
2 large pinches saffron
1 tsp. ground cumin
5 bay leaves
2 Tbs. dry oregano
1 qt. chicken stock
kosher salt to taste
fresh black pepper to taste

2 cups Italian parsley, minced
3 cups artichoke bottoms, cubed
1 cup green olives, pitted and minced
1/2 cup dried apricots, julienne
1/2 cup preserved lemons, soaked and diced (optional)

PREPARATION

Preheat oven to 375 degrees. In large Dutch oven or stovetop-safe tajine, brown seasoned lamb in batches, making sure not to crowd the pot. Add onions, garlic, and spices. Cook until onions are translucent, about 10 minutes. Add chicken stock. Cover and bake 1-1/2 hours. After that time, add remaining ingredients and bake 25 minutes uncovered. Season to taste. Serve with couscous or rice, with favorite hot sauce or chutney on the side.

SERVES 6

SCHNEITHORST'S

BAKED FISH RED SNAPPER À LA CREOLE

Ingredients
1 (8-oz.) red snapper fillet per serving
melted butter
salt to taste
Creole sauce (see below)
lemon wedges and parsley

PREPARATION

Preheat oven to 350 degrees. Place snapper fillets on an oiled sheet pan. Brush them with melted butter and bake for about 20 minutes. Remove the fish from the oven. Arrange the fillets on a serving dish and top with the Creole sauce. Add salt to taste and garnish with lemon wedges and parsley.

Creole Sauce Ingredients
6 Tbs. olive oil
2 medium onions, thinly sliced
3 cloves garlic, crushed
3 cups finely cut peeled and seeded ripe tomatoes or 1 (33-oz.) can Italian plum tomatoes
1/2 cup green pepper, finely chopped
2 Tbs. fresh thyme or tarragon or 1-1/2 tsp. dry thyme or tarragon
1 tsp. salt or to taste
1 tsp. fresh ground pepper
1 tsp. sugar
1/2 cup tomato paste
1/4 cup fresh Parmesan cheese, grated

Sauté the onion and garlic in the oil. Add the tomatoes, green pepper, thyme or tarragon, salt, pepper and sugar and simmer for 30 minutes. Add the tomato paste, stir well and simmer for another 10 minutes. Add the cheese and mix thoroughly, then correct seasoning. Serve over fish.

SAUERBRATEN WITH GRAVY AND POTATO PANCAKES

Sauerbraten Ingredients
1-1/2 lbs. beef shoulder
1/2 cup vinegar
1/2 cup water
1 onion, sliced
salt and pepper to taste
1 bay leaf
1 clove garlic
1 marrow bone
2 Tbs. fat (bacon drippings or lard)
1 onion, sliced
1 tomato, peeled and sliced
Sauerbraten Gravy (see recipe)

PREPARATION

Place beef in a large bowl. Bring the vinegar and water to a boil and add the sliced onion, salt and pepper, bay leaf and garlic. Pour the marinade over the beef. Cover and refrigerate 2-3 days. Remove the meat and dry thoroughly with paper towels. Reserve the marinade. In a heavy kettle heat the fat, and then add the meat and marrow bone and brown on all sides. Add the onion, tomato and 1/2 cup of the marinade. Cover tightly and simmer gently until the meat is tender, about 1 hour. Turn the meat in remaining liquid so that it is coated on all sides. Remove the meat to a warm platter and keep hot while preparing the gravy. To serve sauerbraten, slice the meat evenly and place the slices slightly overlapping on a hot platter. Coat with some of the sauce and serve the rest separately. Serve with potato pancakes.

Sauerbraten Gravy Ingredients
1 Tbs. flour
vinegar or lemon juice
pinch of sugar
salt
butter
cream or wine

Mix flour with pan liquid until smooth. Add the rest of the marinade and stir until smooth and thickened. Sauerbraten sauce calls for more ample ingredients than other sauces. Add, to taste, a little vinegar or lemon juice, a pinch of sugar, salt, a little fresh butter and a Tbs. of cream or wine. Strain and pour over meat or serve as a separate sauce. Note: The sauce should be pungent, with just a suspicion of sweetness. In some parts of Germany, sour cream is used instead of wine.

Potato Pancakes Ingredients
2 lbs. potatoes, peeled
1 lb. onions, peeled
juice of 1 lemon
2 eggs
1/4 tsp. salt
1/8 tsp. pepper
1/4 cup all purpose flour
1/4 cup matzo meal
3/4 cup salad oil

Preheat oven to 375 degrees. Grind or grate the potatoes and onions together and add the lemon juice to prevent discoloration. Let stand 5 minutes, and then drain off excess liquid. Add eggs, salt, pepper, flour, matzo meal. Heat oil and then drop batter onto hot oil. When bottoms are brown, flip.

SEVEN GABLES INN

GONE BUT NOT FORGOTTEN Sterling Hotels & Resorts

CHICKEN BOZADA

Ingredients
4 (6-oz.) chicken breasts
1/2 cup Italian breadcrumbs
1/4 cup toasted pine nuts
juice of one lemon
1/4 cup fresh parsley, chopped
5 sprigs fresh rosemary
2 cups 40% cream
1 cup dry sherry
1 Tbs. salt
1/2 Tbs. ground black pepper
1/3 cup fresh garlic, chopped
1/3 cup olive oil

PREPARATION

Season chicken breasts with salt and pepper. Grill chicken until done and set aside. In medium saucepan, sauté garlic with salt and pepper in olive oil for 3-4 minutes. Do not allow to brown. Add sherry. Boil for 3-4 minutes. Add one rosemary sprig, lemon juice and cream. Cook until thick and creamy, and then remove rosemary.

Remove to a platter and keep warm. Pool sauce on 2 plates. Sprinkle breadcrumbs on chicken; lightly brown under broiler. Place 2 breasts on each plate. Top with pine nuts, and garnish with chopped parsley and fresh rosemary. Serve with choice of side dish. We at the Seven Gables Inn serve Chicken Bozada with pasta. Also, we recommend a Chardonnay from California to accompany this dish.

OYSTER POORBOYS

The Truffle Aioli Ingredients
3 egg yolks
1 whole egg
1 oz. white wine vinegar
2 tsp. dry mustard
21 oz. vegetable oil
3 oz. truffle oil
salt and pepper to taste
1 oz. lemon juice

The Sun-dried Tomato, Arugula, and Bread Ingredients
12 sun-dried tomatoes, reconstituted in water
12 pieces of arugula
12 pieces of white bread cut into 1-inch squares and toasted

The Parsley Jus Ingredients
2 bunches flat leaf parsley, blanched and then shocked in ice bath (see preparation)
3 oz. vegetable oil
1 oz. truffle oil
salt to taste

The Oysters Ingredients
12 blue point oysters, shucked
6 oz. flour
1/2 oz. cayenne pepper
1 qt. vegetable oil
salt and pepper to taste
candy thermometer

PREPARATION

For the truffle aioli, combine yolks, vinegar, and mustard in a food processor and pulse. Gradually add the vegetable oil until fully incorporated and thick. Drizzle truffle oil into mayonnaise. Add salt and pepper to taste then lemon juice, and refrigerate.

For tomato, arugula, and bread, cut and toast bread. Re-hydrate sun-dried tomato in water or olive oil heated about 20 minutes. Put aside arugula in a container.

For parsley jus, boil water in a pot and blanch parsley leaves for 15 seconds then shock in an ice bath. In a blender, add parsley leaves and pulse. Slowly drizzle vegetable oil until incorporated, then truffle oil. Add a pinch of salt and reserve.

For the oysters, use a candy thermometer and heat vegetable oil in a pot to 325 degrees. Combine flour with cayenne. Dredge oysters in flour mix and place in fry pot. With a slotted spoon, remove after browned and exterior is crunchy (approximately 45-60 seconds). Place on a plate with paper towels and season with salt and pepper.

To assemble: spread truffle aioli, sun-dried tomatoes, and arugula on toasted bread. Place a fried oyster on top, then a dollar-size amount of truffle aioli. Garnish with parsley jus and serve.

SERVES 6

BOW TIE PASTA WITH ROQUEFORT CRÈME SAUCE

Ingredients
1/4 lb. bow tie pasta, cooked *al dente*
1 cup half and half
2 tsp. garlic
1/4 cup Roquefort, crumbled
2 oz. mushrooms, sliced
10 leaves of spinach
2 tsp. Parmesan cheese
4 oz. chicken breast, grilled and diced
salt and pepper to taste

PREPARATION

Bring half and half to boil; lower heat. Add garlic, salt and pepper. Add pasta and stir gingerly. As crème sauce begins to thicken, add mushrooms and spinach. While stirring gingerly, add Roquefort and Parmesan cheeses. Remove from heat, stirring in cheeses. Place on plate with uniform texture. Evenly garnish with diced chicken breast on top and serve.

SOULARD'S RESTAURANT & BAR

1731 S. 7th St. 314-241-7956 www.soulards.com

PEPPERED PORK TENDERLOIN

Ingredients
2 whole pork tenderloins
1 cup mayonnaise
1/2 cup sour cream
1/3 tsp. salt
1/3 tsp. white pepper
1/2 tsp. garlic powder or 1/2 tsp. pressed garlic
3 tsp. Dijon mustard
3 tsp. Worcestershire sauce

Ingredients for Marinade
2 cups vegetable oil
1/3 cup soy sauce
1/4 cup honey
1 tsp. onion powder
1 tsp. garlic powder
seasoned salt to taste
cracked pepper to taste

PREPARATION

For the sauce, mix mayonnaise, sour cream, salt, white pepper, garlic, mustard and Worcestershire sauce. Refrigerate until needed.

For the marinade, combine oil, soy sauce, honey, onion powder, and garlic powder in a metallic bowl that is large enough to hold meat.

Trim the tenderloins for fat. Put meat in marinade; let marinate, refrigerated, for at least 6 hours, turning meat occasionally. Remove meat from marinade. Discard marinade. Sprinkle both sides of meat with seasoned salt and pepper. Use a generous amount of pepper because some of the pepper falls off during grilling.

Remove sauce from refrigerator while grilling meat and let it come to room temperature. Grill meat over hot coals or put meat on broiler pan and broil for 3-4 minutes on each side. Slice each piece of meat crosswise into 6-8 slices, each about 3/4-inch thick. Return slices to grill or broiler. Cook to desired doneness, about 4-5 minutes.

Arrange medallions (tenderloins) on serving plate. Serve with sauce.

Note: Marinade yields twice as much as needed. May be saved and used on pasta or rice served with tenderloin. If not desired, cut marinade recipe in half.

SOUTHERN BELLE SUPPER CLUB MEATLOAF

Ingredients
2 lbs. ground beef
2 cups Japanese breadcrumbs
1/2 cup water
1/3 cup onions, chopped
1/3 cup green pepper, chopped
1/3 cup red pepper, chopped
2 eggs
2 tsp. beef base
1/4 tsp. black pepper
2 tsp. Worcestershire sauce
4 tsp. Frank's Red Hot Sauce

Brown Sauce Ingredients
4 Tbs. meatloaf drippings (oil only)
4 Tbs. all purpose flour
2 cups beef broth
1/2 tsp. salt
1/4 tsp. pepper

PREPARATION

Heat oven to 350 degrees. Put all ingredients in a suitable sized bowl. Mix well. Pour meatloaf into a 9 x 5-inch loaf pan. Level the top with a spoon. Bake for 1-1/2 hours. Let meatloaf stand for 5 minutes after cooked. Pour off excess drippings. Loosen with a spatula from loaf pan. Lift meatloaf out with 2 spatulas onto a warm platter, topside up. Top with brown sauce. Serve with green beans and mashed potatoes.

SERVES 8

ST. LOUIS STEAKHOUSE IN HISTORIC COURT SQUARE

GONE BUT NOT FORGOTTEN

LOBSTER-STUFFED VEAL CHOP WITH A LOBSTER BEURRE BLANC

Ingredients
16-oz. veal chop, loin cut
6 oz. lobster meat
1 egg
1 oz. fresh dill
1 oz. fennel fronds
1 oz. fennel, minced
1 oz. shallot, minced
1 oz. garlic, minced
1 oz. chervil, chopped
3 oz. Boursin cheese
1 oz. cognac
2 oz. panko breadcrumbs (Japanese breadcrumbs)
salt and pepper to taste

PREPARATION

Combine all ingredients to make stuffing. No cooking required for this step.

Lobster Beurre Blanc Ingredients
2 oz. shallots, minced
1 oz. fennel, minced
1 oz. leeks, chopped
1 oz. paprika
1/4 cup sherry wine vinegar
1/4 cup cognac
2 cups lobster stock (lobster base can be substituted to make stock)
1 cup 40% cream or heavy cream
1 cup unsalted butter
1 cup shaved fennel
3 cups olive oil for frying

For the sauce, sweat shallots, fennel and leeks in medium saucepan for about 5 minutes. Add paprika and cook for one minute. Then add sherry wine vinegar and reduce until almost evaporated. Add cognac and reduce by one-third. Add cream and then reduce by half. Remove from heat and slowly whisk in butter. Strain through fine colander and keep warm.

For the veal, pan sear veal chop in olive oil until rare. Remove from skillet and let rest. Slit pocket in fat side of veal chop. Pack 3 oz. of stuffing into the pocket. Place in 450-degree oven for 8-10 minutes. (This will be at about medium rare to medium.) Plate and arrange sauce under veal chop and garnish with chopped chervil.

CHICKEN CARCIOFI

Ingredients
4 (6-oz.) boneless skinless chicken breasts
4 slices provel cheese
1 can artichoke hearts
4 Tbs. olive oil
2 Tbs. butter
2 garlic cloves, crushed
1/4 small onion, finely diced
1/2 cup Chablis
1 cup chicken stock
6 mushrooms, sliced 3/16 inches thick
juice of 1/2 lemon
1/8 cup chopped parsley

PREPARATION

Pound chicken breast lightly and dust with flour. In a skillet, sauté the chicken in the olive oil and butter until golden brown. Remove chicken from skillet and set aside. Add garlic and onion and sauté until translucent. Remove excess oil and add wine, 1/2 cup chicken stock, artichoke hearts, mushrooms, lemon juice, and salt and pepper to taste. Cook for 2 minutes.

Return chicken breasts to skillet, top each breast with one piece of artichoke heart and then top the artichoke heart with one slice of cheese. Cover skillet and cook for 1 minute until cheese melts over the artichoke heart and chicken breast. Sprinkle with parsley and add more chicken stock as needed; skillet should be juicy.

Now you are ready to serve. Place one chicken breast on each plate and top each with sauce from skillet.

SERVES 4

SYDNEY'S

GONE BUT NOT FORGOTTEN

By Chef Richard Perry

SEAFOOD CIOPPINO

Ingredients
8 dried pasillo chile peppers
1/4 cup olive oil
4 cups onion, diced
4 cups corn kernels
1/4 cup boiled garlic, minced
4 cans cannelini beans (15-oz. cans)
4 cans diced tomatoes, undrained
32 oz. seafood broth or clam juice
4 cups white wine
4 cups water
1/2 cup green chiles, diced
4 tsp. salt
2 tsp. chili powder
1/4 cup olive oil
4 lbs. orange roughy, cut into 1-inch pieces
4 lbs. monkfish, cut into 1-inch pieces
2 lbs. shrimp

PREPARATION

Soak the pasillo peppers in boiling water for 20 minutes. Remove and reserve 1/4 cup of the water. Remove the seeds and stems from the peppers; blend the peppers with the liquid until smooth. Combine the pasillo pepper, olive oil, corn kernels, minced garlic, cannelini beans, diced tomatoes, clam juice, white wine, water and green chiles. Simmer for 20 minutes; season with salt and pepper. Combine the chili powder and salt; sprinkle over the fish and shrimp. Par-cook the fish and shrimp in the olive oil, then chill. To serve, add the fish and shrimp to the liquid and heat through.

TANNER B'S CHICKEN POT PIE IN SOURDOUGH BREAD BOWL

Ingredients

4 stalks celery, diced
3 medium carrots, diced
1 large yellow onion, diced
2 Tbs. vegetable oil

4 (6-oz.) boneless chicken breasts, cubed
1 (15-oz.) can sweet kernel corn
7 oz. frozen peas, thawed
1 Tbs. thyme
2 tsp. white pepper
2 tsp. salt
2 Tbs. rosemary
1 cup milk
1 cup heavy whipping cream
4 5-inch round sourdough rolls

PREPARATION

Heat vegetable oil in large saucepan. Add celery, onion and carrots. Cook until onion becomes translucent, stirring frequently. Add cubed chicken breast, stirring frequently until chicken is cooked. Add thyme, white pepper, salt and rosemary. Cook for 1 minute, stirring constantly. Add corn, peas, milk and heavy whipping cream. Simmer for 30 minutes, stirring every 7-8 minutes.

While pot pie is simmering, hollow out sourdough rolls, putting top of roll aside. Fill each sourdough roll with the pot pie mix and serve with the top of roll on the side for dipping.

TERRA COTTA GRILL

4 N. Central Ave. 314-721-8889 www.terracottagrill.com

PAINTED DESERT QUESADILLA, WITH SALMON & HERB CHEESE

Ingredients
4 (12-inch) garlic herb wraps, or 12-inch flour tortillas
12 oz. smoked salmon
6 oz. Boursin cheese
3 cups shredded jack cheese
6 cups baby spinach, washed, and stems removed
cooking spray for grilling
1 Tbs. butter
salt and pepper
nutmeg
garlic

PREPARATION

Season spinach with butter, salt and pepper, nutmeg, and garlic. Cover with plastic wrap and sweat quickly in microwave (don't overcook spinach). Uncover and stir. Spread Boursin cheese on herb wraps. Divide salmon, shredded cheese, and spinach between the herb wraps. Fold in half and place on a heated griddle. Flip quesadilla when cheese begins to melt. Grill until crisp on both sides. Serve with cool ranch cream, red pepper oil, and yellow tomato salsa.

Cool Ranch Mayo Ingredients
1/2 cup ranch dressing
1/2 cup sour cream
salt and pepper
pinch or chopped parsley

Mix all ingredients together.

Red Pepper Oil Ingredients
2 roasted red peppers
1/4 cup red wine vinegar
1 Tbs. honey
3/4 cup olive oil
1 Tbs. red onion, chopped
1 tsp. garlic, chopped
1 tsp. chipotle, puree
salt and pepper

Puree all except oil and salt and pepper. Add oil while blending until emulsified. Season with salt and pepper.

Yellow Tomato Salsa Ingredients
4 cups yellow tomatoes, diced
1 tsp. minced garlic
2 serrano chilis, seeded and chopped
1/4 cup cucumber, peeled, seeded, and diced
2 Tbs. cilantro, chiffonier cut
1/2 cup minced red onion
2 Tbs. rice wine vinegar
2 Tbs. lime juice
pinch of sugar

Chop finely in food processor and refrigerate two hours.

TONY MARINO'S

PASTA PORTOBELLO

Ingredients
6 oz. cooked penne pasta
1/2 cup portobello mushrooms, sliced into strips
1 Tbs. sun-dried tomatoes
1/2 cup fresh spinach
1 Tbs. fresh basil, chopped
2 tsp. garlic, chopped
1 tsp. shallots, chopped
2 oz. olive oil
1 oz. Chardonnay
1 oz. chicken stock
salt and pepper to taste.
Parmigiano, shaved

PREPARATION

Sauté garlic, shallots, basil, spinach, and mushrooms in olive oil for 2 minutes. Add stock and wine. Sauté for 3 minutes. Add cooked penne pasta and simmer for 5 minutes. Remove from heat. Place in bowl and top with freshly shaved Parmigiano.

TORNATORE'S RISTORANTE

CHICKEN PICCATA

Ingredients
4 (6-8 oz.) boneless skinless chicken breasts, slightly pounded
pinch of fresh garlic, chopped
1/4 tsp. shallots, chopped
1 tsp. capers
1/4 cup fresh shiitake mushrooms, sliced
1/4 cup white wine
1/2 lemon, freshly squeezed
1 Tbs. butter
1 Tbs. fresh parsley, chopped

PREPARATION

Lightly flour chicken breast and sauté in butter. Brown chicken on both sides. Add garlic, shallots, mushrooms and capers. Add white wine and lemon juice. Take breasts out of skillet and reduce sauce until thickened. Add parsley and serve over chicken breasts.

SERVES 4

TRAINWRECK SALOON

9243 Manchester Rd. 314-962-8148
314 Westport Plaza 314-434-7222
720 N. 1st St. 314-436-1006

STUFFED CHICKEN BREAST

Stuffing Ingredients
7 oz. double-lobe chicken breasts
Parmesan cheese
provolone cheese, shredded
bleu cheese crumbles
fresh spinach, chopped
Italian breadcrumbs
skewers or toothpicks

Sauce Ingredients
4 oz. prepared chicken stock
3 oz. white wine
1 tsp. garlic, chopped
1/2 cup mushrooms, sliced
1 Tbs. butter

PREPARATION

Pound out chicken breast between 2 sheets of film wrap. Prepare stuffing mix as follows: 2 parts provolone cheese, 1/2 part Parmesan cheese, 1/4 part bleu cheese, 1 part spinach. Blend cheese and spinach together to form stuffing. Roll stuffing in chicken breast and secure with skewers or toothpicks. Dust chicken in breadcrumbs and charbroil on all sides.

Remove skewers and top with sauce. Serve with starch and vegetable. For the sauce, place chicken stock, white wine, garlic, and butter in small skillet and heat on medium. Heat until sauce reduces and thickens. Add mushrooms and heat through.

TRATTORIA BRANICA

10411 Clayton Rd. 314-432-8585

FETTUCCINE GENOVESI

Ingredients
1/2 lb. fresh fettuccine
1/4 cup sun-dried tomatoes
2 Tbs. pine nuts
1/2 cup mushrooms
1 tsp. fresh garlic, minced
1 pt. 40% heavy cream
3 Tbs. grated Parmesan

PREPARATION

Heat oil and add garlic until golden brown. After 5 minutes, add mushroom, pine nuts and sun-dried tomatoes. Add cream and bring to a boil. Add freshly cooked fettuccine. Toss together 3 minutes and add Parmesan cheese.

TRATTORIA MARCELLA

3600 Watson Rd. 314-352-7706

LOBSTER RISOTTO

Ingredients
2 cups Arborio rice
2 Tbs. olive oil
7 Tbs. sweet butter
1/4 small yellow onion, diced
2 cups assorted mushrooms, sliced
1/2 Tbs. garlic, minced
88 oz. lobster or shrimp stock
6 oz. tomato sauce
1/2 cup 40% cream
2 cups fresh baby spinach
1 cup Reggiano cheese, grated (optional)
salt and pepper, 3 good pinches or to taste
2 (1-lb.) lobsters, steamed and shelled

PREPARATION

Sauté onions in olive oil and butter until translucent. Add mushrooms until soft. Add rice, garlic, salt, and pepper. Sauté until garlic is slightly toasted. Add all tomato sauce, cream, and stock to cover the rice. Slowly stir and add stock as needed. When rice is nearly cooked, add lobster meat, spinach and cheese. Check for proper consistency, seasoning and doneness of rice.

TURVEY'S ON THE GREEN

CASHEW-ENCRUSTED TUNA WITH JASMINE RICE AND PLUM SAUCE

Ingredients
2 (6-8 oz.) tuna fillets, yellow fin or ahi
1 cup cashews
1 cup Japanese breadcrumbs (panko crumbs)
1/2 cup flour, seasoned with salt and pepper

Plum Sauce
1 (6-8 oz.) jar Asian-style plum sauce
4 cloves garlic, minced
2 shallots, minced
12 oz. seafood stock
1/2 cup brandy

PREPARATION

Finely chop the cashews, and then mix with the breadcrumbs. Lightly dust the tuna fillet in flour, and then in an egg wash (egg and milk). Next coat with cashew and bread crumb mixture. Pan fry on each side on medium high heat until golden brown on both sides.

In a saucepot, lightly sauté the minced garlic and minced shallots in olive oil until they soften slightly. Add the brandy (Be careful! Brandy is very inflammable so give yourself plenty of space). Allow the brandy to reduce until gone, and then add the seafood stock and plum sauce. Simmer for 15 minutes until the sauce lightly coats the back of a spoon. Serve with steamed jasmine rice.

SERVES 2

WASHINGTON AVENUE BISTRO

827 Washington Ave. 314-418-5750

BISTRO PORK TENDERLOIN
WITH POTATO PANCAKES & HOMEMADE APPLESAUCE

Ingredients
4 each tenderloins of pork
Season pork with salt and pepper

PREPARATION

Heat 2 oz. of butter in medium sauté pan to near smoke point. Pan sear pork tenderloins until golden brown. Set in a 350-degree oven for 14 to 16 minutes until cooked to 145 degrees.

Potato Pancakes Ingredients
1 cup Idaho potatoes, grated
1 cup white onion
1 Tbs. flour
1 whole egg
Pinch nutmeg, salt and white pepper
2 Tbs. oil

Peel and grate potatoes and onion. Mix one Tbs. of flour and one whole egg until fully incorporated. Season with salt, white pepper, and nutmeg. Heat a skillet to 350 degrees; add oil and sauté until golden brown. Finish with salt and pepper to taste.

Balsamic Reduction
2 cups balsamic vinegar
1 Tbs. honey to taste
1 Tbs. cornstarch mixed with 1 Tbs. cold water (slurry)

Reduce balsamic vinegar by half volume and thicken with cornstarch slurry.

Apple Sauce Ingredients
10 Granny Smith apples
1 cup apple cider
1 cup sugar
1 tsp. cinnamon
1/4 tsp. nutmeg

Simmer 2 cups shredded apples with one cup each sugar and apple cider until cooked soft. One each Granny Smith apple, peeled, cored and diced, sautéed in 1 oz. of butter until caramelized. Add cinnamon and nutmeg. Add applesauce with sautéed apples. Hold warm until service time. Serve with braised baby spinach, or German-style purple cabbage.

SERVES 4

YEMANJA BRASIL RESTAURANTE

2900 Missouri Avenue 314-771-7457 www.brazildining.com

FREELOAD

Ingredients
2 1/4 lbs. black beans
1 lb. Portuguese sausage
1-1/3 lbs. smoked pork ribs
2-1/4 lbs. Brazilian dried beef
4 cloves garlic
4 onions, diced
1 bay leaf
5 bunches cilantro
Olive oil

PREPARATION

Cook black beans for 1 hour with plenty of water, bay leaf, and cilantro. Add the sausage, beef and ribs.

In a separate frying pan, sauté garlic and onions, then add to the pot of black beans. Cook for 40 minutes. Serve with white rice, slices of fresh oranges, and sautéed collard greens.

SERVES 8

XIN XIM DE GALINHA

Chicken Filet, sautéed with spicy "vatapa" sauce (coconut cream blended with red pepper, sweet peppers, ground cashew, peanuts and shrimp), served over rice

Ingredients

4 lbs. fish
2 lbs. fresh shrimp
1 lb. dried shrimp
8 (8-oz.) boneless chicken breasts
3 large onions, chopped
6 large tomatoes, diced
2 red bell peppers, diced
1 lb. bread
4 cups fish stock
2 cups coconut milk
5 Tbs. dende oil (red palm oil)
1-1/2 cups cashews, diced
1-1/2 cups roasted peanuts, diced
4 cloves garlic, minced
1/2 bunch of cilantro and/or parsley, chopped
2 bay leaves
2 tsp. fresh ginger, grated
Salt, black pepper, malagueta pepper to taste
cooked rice

PREPARATION

Vatapa Sauce:

Sauté 2 chopped onions, 2 minced garlic cloves, red bell peppers, and tomatoes in 1 Tbs. dende oil. Add fish and shrimp to sauté. Pour in enough fish stock to cover. Simmer on a low heat until fish can be flaked apart. While seafood is simmering, soak bread in enough coconut milk to moisten bread. In a blender or food processor, blend together remaining onions, garlic, peanuts, cashew nuts, dried shrimp and ginger. Pour into a large mixing bowl and set aside. In a blender or food processor, blend the moistened bread to a smooth paste and add to mixture; stir until well combined. With the remaining dende oil and coconut milk, pour in a large cooking pan and bring to a boil. Add the remaining fish stock and reduce heat to a simmer. Add sauté seafood mixture and bread mixture to the dende oil, coconut milk, and fish stock.

Main Dish:

Sauté the boneless chicken breasts until golden brown. Serve chicken breast on top of bed of cooked rice. Top chicken and rice with the Vatapa sauce.

SERVES 8

ZIA'S "ON THE HILL"

5256 Wilson Ave. 314-776-0020 www.zias.com

PASTA ALBANELLA

Ingredients
2 oz. butter
1 oz. brandy
1/2 qt. heavy cream
3 oz. mushrooms
1 small shallot
2 oz. Parmesan
6 jumbo shrimp
8 oz. linguine

PREPARATION

Cook pasta and set aside, coating noodles lightly in oil. Sauté shrimp, shallots, and mushrooms in the butter for about 3 minutes. Add the brandy and heavy cream. Bring the mixture to a boil and add the pasta. Bring mixture back to a boil, add Parmesan and toss until the cheese has blended into the cream.

CAPELLINI LORENZO

Ingredients
1-1/2 tsp. fresh garlic, chopped
1/4 tsp. crushed red pepper flakes
1 tsp. each salt and pepper mix
1 tsp. basil
1 oz. olive oil
1 oz. clarified butter
2 oz. sun-dried tomatoes
2 oz. tomato sauce
5 oz. fresh tomatoes, diced
3 oz. fresh mushrooms, sliced
4 oz. shrimp, any size
1 oz. chicken stock
5 oz. capellini noodles
fresh Parmigiana, grated

PREPARATION

In a large sauté skillet, combine olive oil, butter, spices, sun-dried tomatoes, fresh sliced mushrooms, fresh diced tomatoes, and shrimp and cook until shrimp is done. Then add tomato sauce and chicken stock. Have the capellini noodles already cooked and add to the skillet. Toss in skillet until everything is mixed in well with the capellini. Pour into serving dish and top with freshly grated Parmigiana.

SERVES 1

ZU ZU'S PETALS

BRONZED SEA BASS OVER COUSCOUS, ARTICHOKE, TOMATO-CAPER RELISH

Ingredients
6 (7-oz.) pieces Chilean Sea Bass
1 lb. couscous
1 cup apple juice
1 cup water
6 oz. tomato caper relish (recipe below)
1/2 green pepper, finely diced
1/2 red bell pepper, finely diced
5 oz. toasted pine nuts
2 Tbs. and 1 tsp. olive oil

PREPARATION

For the couscous, bring water and apple juice to a boil; pour over couscous in a mixing bowl. Cover with plastic and wait 7 minutes; then fluff with a fork. Toss pine nuts with 1 tsp. of olive oil. Toast in a pre-heated oven about 3 minutes. Mix couscous and toasted pine nuts together with the finely diced bell peppers. Set aside.

Tomato Caper Relish Ingredients
2 roma tomatoes, finely diced
6 green olives, thinly sliced
2 artichoke crowns, thinly sliced and blanched
1 Tbs. drained capers
1 tsp. red wine vinegar
1/4 tsp. paprika
1/4 tsp. cracked black pepper
1/4 tsp. minced garlic

Mix together and set aside. To cook sea bass, in a large skillet heat 2 Tbs. olive oil. Place sea bass in the skillet to brown. Turn bass and place in preheated 350-degree oven for 4-5 minutes.

To serve Bronzed Sea Bass over Couscous:

Fill a coffee cup with couscous, pack tightly, invert on a plate and tap edge of cup on plate to empty cup. The couscous should be in the shape of the cup. Place sea bass on plate with one corner of fish on the couscous. Top with the reserved tomato caper relish.

SAUCES

ANNIE GUNN'S

16806 Chesterfield Airport Rd. 636-532-7684

CABERNET CRACKED PEPPER BUTTER

Ingredients
1 lb. unsalted butter
2 Tbs. garlic, minced
2 Tbs. shallots, minced
1 Tbs. Worcestershire sauce
1 Tbs. dried thyme
2 Tbs. cracked pepper
2 cups red wine (cabernet)
2 Tbs. honey to finish
1 Tbs. kosher salt

Allow butter to soften at room temperature. Combine ingredients 2 through 7 and reduce until dry in a saucepan on stove. Allow reduced mixture to cool and then combine with butter in mixer and whip for 5 minutes. Finish with salt and honey.

**Goes great on steaks, pork, tuna, salmon and chicken. Just melt on top.

BABALU'S

GONE BUT NOT FORGOTTEN

BABALU'S JAMAICAN RUM & GINGER GLAZE

Ingredients
2 cloves garlic
1 pc. ginger
1 stick cinnamon or 1 tsp. ground cinnamon
1 tsp. ground cloves
1 cup dark or amber rum (Bacardi, Ron Rico, or Capt. Morgan)
1 cup light brown sugar
2 limes, juiced
1 tsp. habeñero pepper sauce
2 Tbs. butter

PREPARATION

Mince the garlic. Peel and finely grate or mince the ginger. Mix these with cinnamon, cloves, rum, brown sugar and lime juice in a small, non-corrosive pot. Bring the mixture to a boil, lower the heat and simmer for 10 minutes. The mixture will become smooth and thick like syrup. Stir in the hot sauce and butter. (For more heat, add additional sauce.)

Whatever meat you are serving, cook until almost done. If grilling or broiling, brush with the glaze, and cook for 1 minute. Continue to baste and turn for 3 or more coatings. (Be careful not to burn the food, because the sugar in the glaze will scorch easily.) If roasting, pour the glaze over the meat and baste with the juices.

The glaze may also be used as a dipping sauce for egg rolls, kebobs or ribs.

CARMINE'S STEAKHOUSE

20 S. 4th St. 314-241-1631 www.lombardosrestaurants.com

GORGONZOLA SAUCE

Ingredients
1 Tbs. clarified butter
2 cups 40% cream
1-1/4 cup red onions, finely chopped
1/3 cup mushrooms, sliced
1/3 cup Gorgonzola cheese, chopped
1/4 cup dry white wine
salt and pepper to taste

PREPARATION

Sauté red onions and mushrooms in clarified butter. Drain off excess. Deglaze with white wine. Add 40% cream and reduce to desired thickness. Add Gorgonzola and salt and pepper to taste.

SERVES 2

EL MUNDO LATINO

4301 Manchester Ave. 314-533-6969 www.thelatinoworld.com

MANGO AND PLANTAIN RELISH

Ingredients
2 green plantains
1 ripe mango
1/2 white onion
1 cup cooked black beans
1 tsp. garlic, chopped
1 lime, juiced
1 lemon, juiced
1/2 cup cilantro, chopped
2 tsp. honey
1/2 cup chopped hominy
salt and pepper to taste

PREPARATION

Place chopped mango, onion and plantain with hominy in food processor. Pulse until minced. Take out and put in bowl. Add remaining ingredients and stir. Place in storage container and put in refrigerator.

SERVES 10 (2-OZ.) SERVINGS

EVEREST CAFETERIA

1916 Washington Ave. 314-621-2021

MANGO CHUTNEY

Ingredients
3 cups ripe mango, cut into small chunks
3 Tbs. tamarind paste
1 cup brown sugar
5 fresh red chiles, minced
1 Tbs. garlic, minced
1 Tbs. ginger, minced
1 tsp. cumin seeds
1 tsp. timur (Szechwan pepper)
1 Tbs. cooking oil
salt to taste

PREPARATION

In a saucepan, heat oil; add cumin seeds and cook until dark brown. Add chiles, garlic, ginger, timur, and salt. Fry for a minute or so. Add mango chunks, tamarind paste and brown sugar. Mix all ingredients well and simmer on low heat for about 30 minutes, or until mango chunks are tender. Remove from heat and let rest to cool.

Puree the mango mixture into a smooth, paste-like mixture. Put in a sterilized, airtight jar and refrigerate.

LLYWELYN'S PUB

4747 McPherson Ave. 314-361-3003 www.llywelynspub.com

LLYWELYN'S WELSH RAREBIT

Ingredients

12 oz. beer
1-1/2 tsp. Worcestershire sauce
2 tsp. dry mustard (Coleman's)
1 lb. cheddar cheese, grated
2 Tbs. cornstarch
1/2 cup milk

PREPARATION

Cook in double boiler until melted. Stir once in a while. Put the cornstarch and milk into a blender and blend quickly. Add hot cheese mixture and blend until smooth. (If you don't use a blender, the texture will be sandy.) If this seems too thick, add some milk.

McGURK'S PUBLIC HOUSE

108 S. Main St., O'Fallon, MO 636-978-9640

ROASTED MUSHROOM SAUCE

Ingredients
2 lbs. prepared mixed mushrooms
3/4 cup dry vermouth/dry white wine
3 whole cloves
1 tsp. salt and pepper
2 sprigs fresh thyme
1 to1-1/2 cups mushroom consommé (reserved from roasted mushrooms)
3 qts. chicken stock
2 chopped shallots
2 oz. olive oil
3 Tbs. chopped garlic or roasted garlic puree
2 cups chopped mixed mushrooms (reserved from roasted mushrooms)
1 cup balsamic vinegar

Combine first five ingredients in a shallow roasting pan. Cover with aluminum foil and roast at high heat until cooked through (approx. 45 minutes). Strain and reserve consommé.

For sauce, combine consommé, chicken stock and shallots. Reduce to 2 quarts. In saucepan or skillet, sauté together olive oil, garlic and chopped mixed mushrooms. Cook until mushrooms begin to release liquid, then deglaze with vinegar and then bring to a boil. Simmer 2-3 minutes and combine with chicken stock reduction. Simmer 10 minutes, adjust seasoning and add remaining roasted mushrooms. May be served as a broth over grilled or roasted meats or thickened slightly with cornstarch or arrowroot and mounted with butter.

NONNA G'S

GONE BUT NOT FORGOTTEN

SUN DRIED TOMATO MUSHROOM BUTTER

Ingredients
2 oz. clarified butter
1 Tbs. minced shallots
2 Tbs. minced garlic
1/2 cup Chablis
1/2 lb. cremini mushrooms, sliced
2 lbs. unsalted butter, softened
1 cup sun dried tomatoes, re-hydrated and chopped
1/2 cup fresh basil, sliced thin
2 dashes Worcestershire sauce
1 tsp. salt
1 tsp. ground white pepper

Heat clarified butter in a large skillet. Add shallots and garlic and sweat until lightly browned. Add mushrooms and sauté briefly. Pour in Chablis and reduce by half. Stir in butter and remove from heat. Mix in sun dried tomatoes, basil, Worcestershire, salt and pepper.

Spread butter into a log shape on parchment paper. Roll up and wrap in plastic wrap.
Label and date. Freeze for up to 3 months. Cut from frozen stage for use.

O'CONNELL'S PUB & GRILL

4652 Shaw Ave. 314-773-6600 www.saucemagazine.com/oconnells

MAYFAIR DRESSING

Ingredients
4 stalks of celery, cleaned and chopped
4 cups olive oil
1 cup apple cider vinegar
4 eggs
4 anchovy filets
1/2 cup heavy mayonnaise
1 Tbs. Grey Poupon mustard
1 Tbs. salt
1 Tbs. garlic, minced or powder
1 Tbs. dry mustard
3/4 cup onions
2 – 3 slices of Swiss cheese

Put all ingredients in blender, except olive oil and mayonnaise. Blend until mixed. Then add mayonnaise and oil. Mix, chill and add to greens and toss.

SERVING 1 BLENDER FULL

ONCE UPON A VINE
GONE BUT NOT FORGOTTEN

CABERNET FIG SAUCE

Ingredients
1/2 bottle Cabernet Sauvignon
7 oz. dried figs
2 cups 40% cream

Poach figs in wine and puree. Add cream, salt and pepper to taste. Heat in saucepan and reduce.

RED CEDAR INN
GONE BUT NOT FORGOTTEN

RED CEDAR INN FRENCH DRESSING

Ingredients
5 1-oz. can tomato soup
3-3/4 cups sugar
5 cups white vinegar
5 tsp. salt
1/4 tsp. pepper
5 tsp. paprika
3-3/4 cups corn oil

Blend first six ingredients well, then add corn oil very slowly and mix well again.

YIELD: 1 GALLON

RIDDLE'S PENULTIMATE CAFÉ & WINE BAR

6307 Delmar Blvd. 314-725-6985 www.riddlescafe.com

RIDDLE'S HOMEGROWN CORN RELISH

Ingredients

5-6 ears homegrown corn
1/2 tsp. ground nutmeg
1 medium red bell pepper
1/2 tsp. dry mustard
1/2 cup green onion, chopped
1/2 tsp. salt
1/2 cup celery, thinly sliced
1/2 tsp. black pepper
2 tsp. fresh basil, minced
1/4 cup sugar
1/4 tsp. cayenne pepper
6 Tbs. tarragon vinegar
1 tsp. ground cumin
1/4 cup olive oil

PREPARATION

Buy freshly picked, homegrown sweet corn on the cob. If corn is not in season, put this recipe away until it is. Shuck the corn, remove the silks and cook in boiling water for 6-8 minutes. Remove the ears to cool. Cut the whole kernels off the cob to measure 2-1/2 cups of kernels.

Chop the green onion, celery and fresh basil. If basil is not in season, neither is corn.

Place the cut corn, chopped green onion, celery and basil in a mixing bowl that is plenty large enough to toss the ingredients. Sprinkle the cayenne, cumin, nutmeg, mustard, salt and pepper over the corn mixture.

In a small saucepan bring the vinegar just to a simmer. Add the sugar, stirring to dissolve. Pour the vinegar/sugar mix directly over the corn mixture and toss well. Next, add the oil to the corn mixture and toss again.

Refrigerate without covering for at least an hour prior to serving to allow the flavors to marry. Serve Riddle's Homegrown Corn Relish as a side dish with sandwiches, on a buffet, or use it as a dressing for thick, juicy slices of homegrown tomato. Keeps well under refrigeration for several days, but chances are it won't last several days.

SUPER SMOKERS BAR-B-QUE

601 Stockell Drive, Eureka, MO, 636-938-9742)

ALL PURPOSE LEMON PEPPER DRY RUB

Ingredients
1 Tbs. lemon pepper
1 tsp. garlic powder
1/4 tsp. cayenne
1/2 tsp. salt
1/2 tsp. sugar

This is a simple yet flavorful spice blend that can be rubbed on meats overnight before they are smoked or grilled. It also works well sprinkled on veggies just before putting them in the oven or on the grill.

Multi-Purpose Simple Marinade Ingredients
14 - to 16-oz. Italian dressing
2 Tbs. chili powder
4 Tbs. lemon juice
1 Tbs. apple cider vinegar
2 Tbs. water

Mix lemon juice, apple cider vinegar, water, and chili powder together. Make sure all cluster lumps are beaten out, so that you get a nice, even distribution. In a bottle, add the above mixture to the Italian Dressing and shake well.

Best if it sits 24 hours before using. This allows the spices to release. The apple cider vinegar and lemon juice give the flavor some citrus tang. Great for marinating pork chops and chicken breasts overnight. Marinate in a dish and cover with plastic wrap tightly.

Here are a couple of rubs I have run across that work well in the back yard. Have fun!

Memphis-Style Rub
1 Tbs. light brown sugar
1 Tbs. white sugar
2 tsp. salt
2 tsp. Accent or MSG
1 tsp. celery salt
1 tsp. ground black pepper
1/4 tsp. cayenne pepper
1 tsp. garlic powder
1 tsp. dry mustard
1 tsp. onion powder

Try this on ribs, pork shoulders, pork chops, or pork tenderloin.

Cajun-Style Rub
1/4 cup salt
2 Tbs. garlic powder
2 Tbs. onion powder
2 Tbs. thyme
2 Tbs. oregano
2 Tbs. paprika
1 Tbs. ground white pepper
1 Tbs. ground black pepper
1-3 tsp. cayenne pepper

Try it on seafood, veggies, or poultry. The cayenne pepper makes this blend hot, so be careful.

SOUPS

ANHEUSER BUSCH COMPANIES

1 Busch Place 314-577-2000

BUDWEISER CHEESE SOUP

Ingredients
3 qts. chicken stock
5 oz. butter or margarine
1/8 cup Worcestershire sauce
1/2 tsp. Tabasco sauce
8 oz. cooked bacon or ham, diced small
5 oz. flour
1/4 cup onion, finely diced
3/4 tsp. garlic salt
1 cup Budweiser beer
20 oz. American cheese, shredded or cubed

PREPARATION

Warm butter in a small saucepan. Add flour and cook for about 5 minutes on low heat, stirring frequently. Set aside. Bring chicken stock to a boil in a large pot. Stir in flour and butter mixture until dissolved. Reduce to low heat and cook for 8-10 minutes, stirring continually to prevent burning. Add onions, Worcestershire, garlic salt, Tabasco sauce, and bacon or ham. Cook on low heat for 30 minutes. Stir in cheese until completely melted. Add Budweiser and cook for about 10 minutes on low heat, stirring frequently, and serve.

YIELD: 1 GALLON

FILÉ GUMBO

Ingredients
1/2 cup oil
3 Tbs. flour
1 lb. andouille sausage, chopped into 1-inch chunks
1 medium white onion, chopped
1 medium green pepper, chopped
1 medium yellow pepper, chopped
1 medium red pepper, chopped
1 Tbs. butter
2 cups chicken broth
1 cup diced chicken, cooked
2 tsp. filé powder
1/2 cup water
salt and pepper to taste
4 cups of rice, cooked

PREPARATION

To make the roux, heat the oil in a saucepan, add the flour and cook stirring constantly until it turns a dark, hazelnut brown color. Set aside.

In another saucepan, sauté the andouille sausage, onion, and peppers in butter until the vegetables are soft. Add the chicken stock and bring to a rolling boil. Add the roux and let simmer for 20 minutes. Add the chicken and season to taste. Dissolve the filé powder in 1/2 cup of water and add to the soup. Simmer for 10 minutes and serve over hot rice.

SERVES 4

MOQUECA

BRAZILIAN FISH CHOWDER

Ingredients
1 yellow onion, minced
6 cloves garlic, peeled and minced
1 cup fresh ginger, peeled and minced
1 cup corn oil
2 cups whole peeled tomatoes, chopped, plus juice
1 can coconut milk
2 cups fish stock or clam juice
1 Tbs. sambal chili paste or red pepper flakes
2 Tbs. lime juice
1 cup cilantro, chopped

2 lbs. combination of any or all of the following:
Assorted firm fish, sea bass, halibut, tuna, shark
Peeled shrimp
Scallops
Mussels
Clams
Lobster

PREPARATION

In a heavy soup pot, sauté onions, garlic and ginger over low heat for 10 minutes. Add tomatoes and their juice and bring to a boil. Add coconut milk and clam juice, return to a boil and simmer 10 minutes. Stir in sambal and lime juice. May be made up to this point, chilled and reheated when ready to finish.

10 minutes before serving, bring the stew sauce back to a simmer. Add in the seafood and simmer until done, about 3-5 minutes, depending on how much you are making. Stir in the cilantro. Serve over rice.

SERVES 4

BLUEBERRY HILL

6504 Delmar Blvd. 314-727-4444

HAMBURGER SOUP

Ingredients
2 lbs. ground chuck
1 Tbs. plus 1 tsp. chopped garlic, divided
2 tsp. ground black pepper (for less spicy use only 1)
1 tsp. celery salt
1 cup onions, chopped
1-1/2 cups celery (including leaves), chopped
2 Tbs. butter or vegetable oil
2 medium potatoes, quartered and cut into 1/2- inch cubes
1 (28-ounce) can chopped tomatoes, un-drained
2-1/2 cups tomato juice
1/4 cup Worcestershire sauce
3/4 tsp. Tabasco sauce
ground red (cayenne) pepper, to taste
8 hamburger buns or dinner rolls

In a skillet, brown the ground chuck with 1 Tbs. garlic, black pepper, and celery salt. Drain. In a large pot, sauté the onions, celery and the remaining garlic in butter until tender. Add the drained meat, potatoes, tomatoes, tomato juice, Worcestershire sauce, Tabasco sauce, red pepper and 1 cup water. Cook over medium heat until soup starts to simmer. Reduce heat and let simmer until potatoes are very tender, about 30 minutes. Serve with hamburger buns or dinner rolls on the side.

SERVES 8, OR 11 CUPS

BLUE WATER GRILL

343 S. Kirkwood Rd. 314-821-5757 www.bluewatergrill.com

MEXICAN BOUILLABAISSE

Ingredients
1 medium yellow onion, sliced thin
16 roma tomatoes, sliced lengthwise
1 (24–32 oz.) can crushed tomatoes
3 Anaheim chile peppers or any type of spicier chile pepper, diced
3 cups of fish stock
1 Tbs. sea salt
1/2 Tbs. oregano
1-1/2 Tbs. garlic, chopped
8 each shrimp, sea scallops, mussels, clams
1 lb. of your choice of seafood cut into small pieces (tuna, halibut, etc.)
1 oz. olive oil
1 tsp. saffron
4 oz. white wine

In a large stockpot, sauté the onions until translucent. Add tomatoes and chile peppers and cook until tomatoes have cooked and released their natural juices. Then add crushed tomatoes, fish stock, salt, oregano and garlic. Simmer for approx. 45 minutes. This can be prepared 2 or 3 days in advance. Next, in a large skillet or pot, heat the olive oil. Sauté shrimp and seafood until medium rare, then add scallops, mussels, clams, saffron and wine. Cook a few minutes and then add the tomato sauce mixture. You will not need all of the sauce – use leftovers for pasta. Serve hot with toasted baguettes.

SERVES 4

CORONADO BALLROOM AND MEETING FACILITY

3701 Lindell Blvd. 314-367-4848 www.thecoronado.com

GOLDEN GAZPACHO

Ingredients
6 large yellow tomatoes, cored
1/2 cucumber, peeled and seeded
1 yellow pepper, seeded
1/2 jalapeño pepper, seeded
1/2 yellow onion
2 stalks of celery
1 Tbs. extra virgin olive oil
1/2 lemon, juiced
1 tsp. sugar
1/2 tsp. cumin, ground
1 tsp. garlic

For Garnish:
2 Tbs. red pepper, diced very small
2 Tbs. green pepper, diced very small
2 Tbs. cucumber
2 Tbs. red onion
2 Tbs. chives
2 Tbs. cilantro
1/3 cup croutons

PREPARATION

Purée in food processor the tomato, cucumber, pepper, jalapeño, onion, celery, garlic and cumin. Chill for 2 hours and then add olive oil, lemon juice, sugar, salt, and pepper to taste.

For garnish, dice peppers, cucumber and red onion, and chop the chive and cilantro. Combine all garnish ingredients in a bowl and mound small amount in center of bowled soup.

FITZ'S RESTAURANT

6605 Delmar Blvd. 314-726-9555 www.fitzsrootbeer.com

FITZ'S CAJUN GUMBO

Our spicy gumbo is made from scratch with clams, scallops, shrimp,
tasso ham and andouille sausage, and topped off with white rice and scallions.

Ingredients
1/4 each red pepper and green pepper, diced
7 carrots, medium diced
1 stalk celery, medium diced
2 medium onions, diced
1 Tbs. thyme
1 Tbs. oregano
1 Tbs. ea. coarse black pepper and Kosher salt
1 Tbs. basil
1 Tbs. granulated garlic
1 Tbs. kosher salt
1 Tbs. cayenne pepper
2 oz. seafood stock
3 medium tomatoes, diced
4 oz. clam juice
16-oz. can clams, drained and chopped
1 Tbs. Worcestershire sauce
1/2 cup flour
1/2 cup butter
1-1/2 lbs. small shrimp, peeled
10 oz. bay scallops, chopped
6 oz. tasso ham, medium diced
6 oz. andouille sausage
4-1/2 cups water

PREPARATION

Add oil to skillet and heat. Add flour to oil and make into a roux. Cook roux to a deep, dark brown
color. Add all diced sausage, ham and vegetables except tomatoes. Let it cook for 10 minutes, stirring
repeatedly. Add tomatoes, clam juice, water, seafood base, and all spices and cook for 5 minutes, stirring repeatedly. Bring to a quick boil and add shrimp, scallops, and clams. Reduce heat and cook for
the final 15 minutes, stirring continuously.

Gumbo is ready once all seafood products are cooked thoroughly. May be garnished with white rice and
scallions.

SERVES 4 WITH LEFTOVERS

GP AGOSTINO'S

15846 Manchester Rd. 636-391-5480

AL MINESTRONE VEGETABLE SOUP

Ingredients
1-1/2 cups dried white beans
2/3 cups olive oil
2/3 cup carrots, thinly sliced
2 cups celery, chopped
2-1/4 cups potato, diced
2 cups plum tomatoes, seeded and chopped
1/2 tsp. dried rosemary
3 medium onions
4 garlic cloves, minced
3 cups freshly cut green beans
4 cups zucchini, diced
10 cups beef stock
Parmesan cheese
salt and pepper to taste

PREPARATION

Place dried beans in bowl with enough water to cover; allow to soak overnight. Heat oil in a large, heavy saucepan, stir in onions and cook for 5 minutes, stirring often. Add garlic until lightly brown. Cook for 2 or 3 minutes, keeping a close eye on it and stirring often. Stir in green beans, zucchini, cabbage, carrot and celery. Cook 8-10 minutes, stirring often to coat mixture with oil. Add 10 cups of beef stock, potato, tomato, salt, pepper, rosemary, and drained beans. Heat to boiling. Reduce heat to low and simmer uncovered or partially covered 3 or more hours. Serve with a generous sprinkle of Parmesan cheese.

HODAK'S RESTAURANT & BAR

2100 Gravois Ave. 314-776-7292 www.hodaks.com

HODAK'S WHITE CHILI

Ingredients
14 cups dried navy beans, soaked overnight
10 chicken breasts
4 onions, diced
26-oz. can diced mild green chiles
5 tsp. ground cumin
2 tsp. red pepper
1/4 cup chicken base
1 tsp. granulated garlic
1/2 tsp. cayenne pepper

PREPARATION

Boil your chicken breasts. Let cool and pull meat off bone. Save chicken stock from breasts. Sauté onions approx. 10 minutes. Stir in garlic, cumin, red pepper, cayenne pepper and chiles. Sauté approx. 2 minutes. Add beans and chicken stock with chicken base. Bring to a boil. Reduce heat and add chicken. Before serving add 5 cups shredded mozzarella. Stir until cheese melts.

J. F. SANFILIPPO'S RESTAURANT

705 N. Broadway 314-621-7213

PESTO SOUP

Ingredients
3 cups vegetable broth
1 cup chicken broth
1/2 cup vermicelli
1/2 cup fresh basil leaves
3 Tbs. pine nuts
3 garlic cloves
1 Tbs. grated Parmesan cheese
2 tsp. olive oil
dash of Worcestershire sauce
salt and freshly grounded black pepper

PREPARATION

In a saucepan, bring both the broths to a boil. Add vermicelli and simmer 10 minutes. Reserve 2 basil leaves and 2 tsp. (10 ml) pine nuts for garnishing. In a food processor, combine remaining basil leaves and pine nuts with garlic, Parmesan and oil. Process. Blend into broth. Simmer 5 minutes.

Meanwhile, finely shred reserved basil leaves. In a bowl, mix with pine nuts. Set aside. Season soup with Worcestershire sauce, salt and pepper. Sprinkle with basil and pine nut garnish. Serve.

JACK CARNEY'S MILLION-DOLLAR CHILI

Ingredients
1/2 lb. pinto beans
5 cups canned tomatoes
1 lb. green bell pepper, chopped
1-1/2 Tbs. vegetable oil
1-1/2 lbs. onions, chopped
2 cloves garlic
1/2 cup fresh parsley, chopped
1/2 cup (1 stick) butter
2-1/2 lbs. ground beef chuck, coarse or chili ground
1 lb. lean ground pork
1/3 cup chili powder
2 Tbs. salt
1-1/2 tsp. pepper
1-1/2 tsp. cumin seed
1-1/2 tsp. MSG

PREPARATION

Wash beans, and then soak overnight in water. In the same water, simmer, covered, until tender. Add tomatoes and simmer 5 minutes. In separate pan, sauté green pepper in oil 5 minutes. Add onion; cook until tender, stirring often. Add garlic and parsley. In another pan, melt butter. Sauté beef and pork for 15 minutes. Add to onion mixture, stir in chili powder; cook 10 minutes. Add meat mixture to beans. Add salt, pepper, cumin and MSG. Simmer, covered, 1 hour. Cook uncovered 30 minutes. Skim fat from top.

KC'S BAR & GRILL

4050 Bamberger 314-664-3035

KC'S FAMOUS POTATO SOUP

Ingredients
5 ribs of celery, diced
1 large yellow onion, diced
8 oz. ham, chopped
1 Tbs. garlic, minced
1 gallon milk
roux of 1 lb. margarine and 2-1/2 cups flour
8 potatoes, peeled, diced and cooked
1 qt. half and half
cheddar cheese, bacon bits and scallions for garnish

PREPARATION

Sauté the vegetables until they are translucent. Add the milk and keep on a medium-low flame until the milk just starts to boil around the edges. Turn off the flame and add the roux with a wire whip until the soup starts to thicken. (It should take all of the roux.) Add the half and half and mix thoroughly. Then fold in the potatoes. Garnish with shredded cheddar cheese, bacon bits and scallions.

SERVES APPROXIMATELY 25 (8 OZ.) SERVINGS

NANTUCKET COVE

GONE BUT NOT FORGOTTEN

NEW ENGLAND CLAM CHOWDER

Ingredients
1 pt. fresh clams, finely chopped
1-1/2 cups strained clam juice
2 medium large potatoes
2 oz. salt pork or slab bacon, rind removed
1 large onion
2 cups whole milk
1/2 cup light cream
1/2 tsp. salt
dash of freshly ground white pepper

PREPARATION

Peel and dice potatoes. Cook in large heavy kettle in just enough water to cover. Don't overcook. Pour off all but 1/2 cup of the potato water.

Dice salt pork and sauté in skillet until crisp and nicely brown. Remove bits with slotted spoon and drain on paper towel. Then sauté finely chopped onion in the pork drippings until soft and translucent, but not brown. Add salt pork, onion and clam juice to potatoes and water. Bring to a boil, reduce heat and simmer for 5 minutes. Gradually stir in milk and cream into hot kettle ingredients. (Do not boil.) Add chopped clams and cook 2 minutes. Season with salt and freshly ground pepper.

NERUDA

4 Club Centre, Ste. A, Edwardsville, IL 618-659-9866

CHILLED CUCUMBER BISQUE

Ingredients
6 cucumbers, peeled and seeded
3 cups buttermilk
4 green onions, chopped
1 cup chicken stock
2 cups sour cream
juice of 2 lemons
1 tsp. fresh dill (to taste)
salt and pepper to taste

PREPARATION

Place the cucumbers and green onions in a food processor. Blend slowly, adding buttermilk until a smooth consistency is achieved. Place mixture in a bowl and add remaining ingredients; whisk and chill.

RIDDLE'S LENTIL & ANDOUILLE SAUSAGE SOUP

Ingredients
1 lb. sliced bacon
1 large yellow onion
3 stalks celery
2 lbs. carrots
2 tsp. fresh garlic, minced
2 lbs. dry green lentils
1 gal. water
1/3 cup beef base
3 Tbs. Maggi seasoning
1 Tbs. sugar
3/4 tsp. dry mustard
1/2 cup parsley, chopped
2 tsp. black pepper
1 tsp. Tabasco sauce
1-1/4 tsp. dry whole thyme
3/4 tsp. granulated garlic
1 lb. andouille sausage*

*Andouille is a Cajun specialty made with ground pork and potatoes. When we started making this soup, nobody in St. Louis sold andouille sausage. It's now pretty widely available, but I recommend you get yours where we get ours—directly from Chef Paul Prudhomme in New Orleans. We've tried a lot of andouilles, and we still use Chef Paul's. You can order by phone at 504-731-3590 or shop on-line at www.chefpaul.com.

While talking to Chef Paul's people, consider ordering a little of his tassos, too. They call it "Cajun ham." Tassos is a lean pork coated with cayenne pepper and smoked. It is outstanding in a cream pasta sauce. They ask if you want "regular" or "hot" andouille. Why call all the way to New Orleans just to get the milder version?

PREPARATION

Cut the bacon into 1-inch pieces. Dice carrots, celery and andouille into 1/2-inch cubes. Mince the garlic and parsley. Gently sauté the bacon right in the bottom of your soup pot, stirring to avoid burning, until some grease is rendered. When the bacon is fairly crisp, add the onion, carrot, celery and fresh garlic. Sauté, stirring until onions are transparent. Add the remaining ingredients except andouille. Bring to a boil; reduce to a simmer for 30-45 minutes. The lentils should be soft but retain their distinctive shape. Add the diced andouille and cook 10 minutes longer.

SURF & SIRLOIN

13090 Manchester Rd. 314-822-3637 www.surfandsirloin.com

CLAM CHOWDER

Ingredients
6 potatoes, cubed
3 cans clams with juice
1 stalk celery, diced
1 Tbs. white pepper
1/3 – 1/2 cup clam base
2 qts. heavy cream
roux
margarine

PREPARATION

Sauté the celery in margarine. Add potatoes, clam juice, white pepper and clam base. Bring to a boil and then add cream. Bring back to boil; add clams and thicken with roux.

TNG'S TWO NICE GUYS

10935 Manchester Rd. 314-821-1800
35 N Gore Ave. 314-968-6440

TNG'S BBQ PULLED PORK CHILI

Ingredients
pork butt (3-5 lbs.)
1 bag kidney beans
4 cups BBQ sauce
1 qt. peeled tomatoes
1/2 qt. water
1/2 cup ketchup
1/4 cup mustard
3 Tbs. cumin
5 Tbs. chili powder
salt and pepper to taste

PREPARATION

Broil pork butt in a 350-degree oven for 1 hour. Soften kidney beans. Simmer other ingredients for 1 hour. Pull pork meat from butt (about 6 cups) and add to pot. Add kidney beans. Simmer for another 15-30 minutes

XANADU

280 Long Rd. 636-532-9262 www.xanaduplace.com

XANADU TURTLE SOUP

Ingredients
1/2 lb. turtle meat
1/2 lb. ground veal or lean ground beef
1 lb. carrots, finely diced
2 ribs celery, finely diced
1 lb. onion, finely diced
1 Tbs. leaf thyme
1 tsp. black pepper
1 Tbs. granulated garlic
4 each chicken and beef bouillon cubes
juice of 1 lemon
1 cup dry sherry
3 qt. water
8 oz. roux to thicken

PREPARATION

Cook turtle meat well and save juice. Grind turtle meat, carrots, celery, onions and other meat. Add turtle juice and all other ingredients to the 3 quarts of water. Cook until done and add sherry. Add roux to thicken.

The end result should be a concentrate that is thinned down to desired thickness when reheating any portion. Thin down with chicken consommé, beef consommé or a little sherry. Since this recipe makes approximately 1 gallon, it can be frozen in small containers, then heated and thinned out before serving.

YIELD: 1 GALLON

DESSERTS

ATLAS RESTAURANT

5513 Pershing Ave. 314-367-6800

ALMOND CAKE

Ingredients
1 lb. butter, unsalted
11 oz. egg whites
15 oz. powdered sugar
10 oz. almond flour
4 oz. pastry flour

PREPARATION

Preheat oven to 350 degrees. Butter 6 tartlet pans. Brown the butter (it should smell nutty). Strain and set aside. With the paddle attachment and a mixer, beat the egg whites and the sugar. Add the almond powder and mix. Add the pastry flour. Stir in the flour slowly. Add the still-warm butter in three parts: Stir in each addition of butter well before adding the next. When all the butter has been added, beat at high speed for 3 seconds.

Fill tartlet pans 2/3 full and bake at 350 degrees until golden brown.

MAKES 6 TARTLETS

BELLA SERA ITALIAN GRILL

11686 Gravois Rd. 314-849-9339

TIRAMISU

Ingredients
1 pkg. imported ladyfingers (the dry ones)
1 qt. heavy cream
1 (16-oz.) tub mascarpone cheese
1 Tbs. pure vanilla
1/2 cup sugar
coffee
3 Tbs. cocoa
4 oz. dark chocolate, shaved
6-7 cups espresso or double-strength coffee
1-1/2 oz. each of these liquors:
Kahlua
Amaretto
Myers Rum

PREPARATION

Place sugar, vanilla and marscapone in mixing bowl and cream together. Set aside.

Whip heavy cream until stiff peaks form. Fold this into marscapone, sugar and vanilla mixture. In a 9 x 11-inch baking dish, spread a thin layer of the cheese/cream mixture on bottom of dish. Dust with cocoa.

Mix coffee and liquors. Quickly dip ladyfingers, 3 or 4 at a time in coffee, then layer closely together on top of cream mixture, covering entirely. Spread approx. half of remaining cheese mixture on top of ladyfingers. Dust with cocoa. Add another layer of coffee-soaked ladyfingers, laying in opposite direction of first layer. Pour any remaining coffee on top of ladyfingers and top with remaining cheese mixture. Dust with cocoa and shaved chocolate. Chill for 3-4 hours.

Slice into 3-in. squares, drizzle with caramel and chocolate and then dive in.

SERVES SIX – EIGHT

CAFE CAMPAGNARD

CHOCOLATE MOUSSE

Ingredients
1 cup whipping cream
2 egg yolks
4 oz. bittersweet chocolate
1/4 cup granulated sugar
1/4 cup water
2 Tbs. cocoa powder
2 Tbs. Grand Marnier, or other orange liqueur
6 Tbs. sour cream
1 Tbs. unsalted butter, softened

PREPARATION

Melt the chocolate, and then cool until just warm. Whip cream to soft peaks. Set aside and keep chilled. Using an electric mixer, beat the yolks until lightly colored. Combine sugar and water and bring to a boil. Boil 90 seconds only. With the motor running, slowly pour the sugar syrup into the yolks. Beat for 5 minutes, or until barely warm.

While yolks are whipping, stir the liqueur into the cocoa. Next stir in the sour cream. Stir this mixture into the chocolate, and then add the butter. When the yolks are finished whipping, fold 1/3 into the chocolate mixture. Fold in the remaining yolks. Fold the reserved whipped cream into the chocolate mixture.

Use immediately. Pour into bowls, glasses or use as a filling for cakes, pies or crêpes.

CAFÉ DE FRANCE

7517 Forsyth Blvd. 314-678-0200 www.saucecafe.com/cafedefrance

APPLE TART TATIN

Ingredients
3 Granny Smith apples, peeled, cored, and cut in half
1/2 lb. whole butter
1/2 lb. granulated sugar
1/2 sheet puff pastry
1 egg, beaten

PREPARATION

In large skillet, combine butter and sugar. Cook on high heat until it begins to brown. Remove from heat and pour directly into 4 tart tins, evenly covering the bottom of each. Slice apple halves into 1/4 inch slices and divide between tart tins in an attractive design. Sprinkle a little additional sugar over apples. Place tarts on sheet pan or cookie sheet. Using extra tart tin, cut 4 circles of puff pastry. Put pastry over apples and tuck into tart tin. Brush egg wash over pastry and poke a few holes into pastry.

Pre-heat oven to 375 degrees. Bake on the center rack for 15-20 minutes, or until pastry is golden brown. Let cool for 10 minutes, then flip tarts over to remove from tins.

SERVES 4

CANNOLI'S RESTAURANT

462 N. Hwy. 67 314-839-5988

ITALIAN COCONUT CREAM CAKE

Ingredients
2 cups sugar
5 egg yolks, beaten
2 sticks butter
2 cups flour
1 tsp. baking soda
1 cup buttermilk
1 cup pecans, chopped
1 cup shredded coconut
1 tsp. vanilla

Cream sugar, egg yolks and butter together. Add flour, baking soda, buttermilk, pecans, coconut and vanilla. Beat egg whites stiff and add to mixture. Put into 13 x 9-inch pan and bake 50 to 55 minutes at 350 degrees. Remove immediately from pan.

Icing
8 oz. cream cheese
1 lb. powdered sugar
1 stick margarine
1-1/2 tsp. vanilla

Mix all ingredients together. Ice cake when completely chilled, and sprinkle on coconut.

CLARK STREET GRILL AT THE WESTIN

811 Spruce Street 314-552-5801

UPSIDE DOWN PEACH POLENTA CAKE

Ingredients
8 ripe peaches
6 oz. soft butter
8 oz. sugar
3 eggs
6 egg yolks
6-1/2 oz. bread flour
5 oz. cornmeal
1 Tbs. baking powder
pinch salt
6 oz. water
6 oz. sugar
2 Tbs. Grand Marnier
1 qt. whipped cream
seasonal fresh berries for garnish

PREPARATION

Bring peaches to a boil for five minutes, and then place in ice water to cool. Using a paddle, mix the butter and sugar until creamy. Slowly add the whole egg and the egg yolks, one at a time. Add all the dry ingredients and mix only until blended. Set aside. On medium heat, caramelize the sugar, water, and Grand Marnier. Spray eight (10-oz.) soufflé dishes with non-stick spray. Cover the bottom of molds with caramel and let set. Cut peaches into sections and lay cut side down in each mold. Spoon polenta batter on top of peaches, filling molds 3/4 full. Bake at 350 degrees for 20 minutes or until solid to the touch. Remove from oven and let cool five minutes before removing from molds. Garnish with fresh berries and whipped cream.

ELIJAH MCLEAN'S RESTAURANT

600 W. Front Street, Washington, MO 636-239-3463

HOUSE SPECIALTY DESSERT

Simple to prepare, this dessert boasts contrasting sweet, tart, and spiced flavors that come together in a visually attractive presentation.

Ingredients
1/2 cup honey
3 Tbs. balsamic vinegar
1/4 tsp. freshly ground black pepper
2 cups peaches, sliced, peeled
2 cups fresh blackberries
pound cake, sliced

Combine honey, vinegar and pepper in a large bowl and whisk thoroughly. Add peaches and berries. Toss gently to coat. Let stand 5 minutes. Serve over slices of basic buttery pound cake and garnish with freshly whipped cream. (May substitute strawberries, nectarines or red plums for blackberries and peaches).

SERVES 6

EVEREST CAFETERIA

1916 Washington Ave. 314-621-2021

KHEER (HIMALAYAN RICE PUDDING)

Ingredients
1 gallon whole milk
2 cups cream
1/2 cup butter
1 cup basmati rice
1 cup sugar
5-6 cardamom
1/4 cup coconut, coarsely shredded
1/4 cup golden raisins
1/2 cup cashews

PREPARATION

In a large cooking pan, heat butter over low heat. Add rice and stir for 2-3 minutes. Pour milk into the rice mixture. Add cream and sugar. Stir thoroughly. Bring to a boil and allow to simmer over low heat, stirring constantly, for about 20 minutes, or until rice has softened.

Add cardamom, coconut, raisins, and cashews and stir well. Cook for another 10 minutes, or until the rice is cooked soft and the mixture has thickened to consistency of your liking. Chill the pudding overnight in refrigerator. Serve with shredded coconut on top.

THE EXCELSIOR CLUB

GONE BUT NOT FORGOTTEN

CHOCOLATE PATÉ "EXCELSIOR"

Ingredients
1-1/4 cup water
2-1/2 cups cane sugar
1-1/4 lb. butter
30 oz. dark chocolate
3/4 cup plus 1 Tbs. cane sugar
3/4 cup plus 1 Tbs. cake flour
12 eggs
1-1/2 cup pecans, finely ground
buttered parchment paper

PREPARATION

Butter 2 large loaf pans and line with buttered parchment paper. Preheat conventional oven to 350 degrees with a deep-water pan. Bring water and 2-1/2 cups sugar to boil (covered, over medium heat) and boil for 2 minutes. Add butter and chocolate, stir until melted and smooth. Beat 1-2/3 cup sugar, flour, and eggs until light and lemon colored.

Add chocolate mixture by hand until completely incorporated. Add chopped pecans and divide into two loaf pans.

Cover top with buttered parchment paper. Bake in a water bath until set. (At least 1-1/2 hours) Cool for 20 minutes and carefully turn out onto a lined baking sheet. Freeze, covered, until ready for use. Slice into thin slices and serve with lightly whipped, unsweetened cream.

GIOVANNI'S LITTLE PLACE

14560 Manchester Rd. 636-227-7230

TIRAMISU

Ingredients
3/4 lb. mascarpone cheese (creamy cheese that is rich and buttery with a smooth texture)
3 Tbs. sugar
1-1/2 cups heavy cream
1/2 cup cold espresso
1/3 cup coffee liqueur
14 ladyfingers
cocoa powder

PREPARATION

Beat the mascarpone and sugar together. Whip the cream until it holds its shape, and then fold it into the mascarpone. Put a few spoonfuls of the mascarpone mixture in the bottom of a serving dish.

Mix the coffee and liqueur in a bowl. Dip 1 ladyfinger in the coffee mixture and turn until just soaked, and then place it on the top of the mascarpone in the dish. Repeat with six more ladyfingers, placing them side by side in the dish.

Cover with half the remaining mascarpone, then soak and layer the remaining ladyfingers. Top with mascarpone and chill for at least 4 hours. Decorate with cocoa powder.

SERVES 4-6

GRAPPA GRILL

1644 Country Club Plaza 636-940-5400

WARM CHOCOLATE TART

Ingredients
1 lb. semi-sweet coverture chocolate
3 oz. unsweetened butter
1 pinch of salt
9 egg yolks
1/2 cup granulated sugar
3 egg whites

PREPARATION

Chop chocolate into small pieces. Melt chocolate, butter and salt over double boiler. Whip egg yolks with 3/4 the amount of sugar to a ribbon consistency. Whip egg whites and remaining sugar to a soft peak. Fold egg yolk mixture into melted chocolate mixture. Fold in 1/3 of egg white mixture. Fold in remaining egg white mixture.

Place in 12-oz. soufflé cups. Place in preheated 400-degree oven and bake 15-20 minutes. Tarts should be slightly underdone for a warm, gooey middle.

HARVEST

1059 S. Big Bend 314-645-3522

BRIOCHE BREAD PUDDING WITH BOURBON CURRANT SAUCE AND VANILLA CREAM

Ingredients

4 loaves brioche, crust removed
2 cups milk
2 cups heavy cream
3/4 cup sugar
1 vanilla bean, split
1 cinnamon stick
1/4 tsp. nutmeg
3 egg yolks
3 eggs
butter, to grease baking dish
2 cups sugar
1/2 tsp. baking soda
1/2 tsp. vanilla
2 Tbs. light corn syrup
1 cup buttermilk
1 cup unsalted butter
1/2 cup bourbon
1 cup currants

PREPARATION

Preheat oven to 350 degrees. Cube the brioche into 1-inch squares and set aside. In a saucepan, combine the milk, cream, sugar, vanilla bean, nutmeg, and cinnamon and bring to a boil. Remove from the heat and quickly whisk in the eggs. Continue whisking until slightly thickened. Do not allow to scramble.

Allow the loose custard to cool slightly, remove the vanilla bean and cinnamon stick and pour over the cubed brioche. Toss lightly and place brioche in a buttered baking dish. Bake for up to 30 minutes or until the top is lightly browned. Remove from the oven and cut into portions.

In the meantime, make the bourbon sauce. Combine the sugar, baking soda, vanilla, corn syrup, buttermilk, and butter in a saucepot and bring to a boil. Simmer for about 20 minutes or until the mixture begins to darken. Add the bourbon and currants and pour over the top of the bread pudding. Serve with vanilla whipped cream.

SERVES 12

ILLINOIS RIVERDOCK
RESTAURANT

310 S. Park, Hardin, IL 618-576-2DOC

POSSUM PIE

Ingredients
4 oz. cream cheese, softened
3/4 cup confectioners sugar
1 (8-inch) graham cracker crust
1/4 cup chopped pecans
1/4 cup instant chocolate pudding mix
1/4 cup instant vanilla pudding mix
1-1/2 cups cold milk
3/4 tsp. vanilla extract
1 cup Cool Whip
12 - 16 pecan halves

PREPARATION

In a mixing bowl, beat cream cheese and sugar until smooth. Spread onto bottom of crust. Sprinkle with chopped pecans. In another mixing bowl, combine pudding mixes.
Add milk and vanilla. Beat on low speed for 2 minutes. Spoon over the pecans.

Refrigerate for at least 2 hours. Top with Cool Whip and pecan halves.

SERVES 6

IRON BARLEY

5510 Virginia Ave. 314-351-4500

APPLE BARLEY PUDDIN

Ingredients
12 cups water
2-1/2 cups (about 1 pound) pearled barley
1/2 cup (1 stick) butter
1/4 cup lemon juice
1 cup honey
1/3 cup packed brown sugar, plus more to taste (see note)
whipped cream, optional
1/2 cup Jack Daniel's Tennessee whiskey, divided (optional)
1-1/3 cups orange juice
8 cups Granny Smith apples, peeled, cored and sliced
2 tsp. ground cinnamon
1 tsp. ground nutmeg
whipped cream

(Cast iron utensils are recommended but not required.) Bring water to a boil in a large pot. Add barley, and reduce to a simmer and cover. Cook for 25 minutes. Preheat oven to 350 degrees.

Meanwhile, heat 12-inch ovenproof skillet, add butter and cook until almost brown. Add apples, stirring occasionally, until liquid is almost gone, (about 5 to 8 minutes). Add brown sugar; cook 2 minutes, stirring occasionally. Add 1/4 cup whiskey and cook until most of the alcohol has evaporated, about 5 minutes. Test sweetness. Stir in additional brown sugar to taste and cook for 2 minutes (see tester's note). Turn off heat.

Strain barley and place in a large bowl. Stir in orange juice, lemon juice, honey, cinnamon, nutmeg and remaining 1/4 cup of whiskey. Spoon barley over apples, level off top, and bake for 25 minutes. Serve with whipped cream.

Tester's note: If using the bourbon, this dish takes on a smoky edge. If you prefer a sweeter dessert, add more brown sugar to taste after you cook in the bourbon.

SERVES 12

JACK CARNEY'S
CHOCOLATE CHIP COOKIES

Ingredients
1/2 cup (1 stick) margarine, softened
1/2 cup solid vegetable shortening
1 cup packed light brown sugar
1 cup granulated sugar
2 eggs, well beaten
1 tsp. vanilla
2 cups all-purpose flour
1 tsp. baking soda
1 tsp. salt
2 cups quick-cooking rolled oats, uncooked
2 cups shredded coconut
8 oz. chopped pecans
2 (12-ounce) packages semisweet chocolate morsels

PREPARATION

With an electric mixer, beat margarine, shortening, brown sugar and granulated sugar until creamy and smooth. Add eggs and vanilla and beat well. Sift together flour, baking soda and salt. Add to batter, mixing well. Stir in oats, coconut, pecans, and chocolate morsels. Stir until well mixed.

Drop dough by well-rounded tablespoons on to an ungreased cookie sheet, allowing space for cookies to spread.

Bake in a preheated 350-degree oven 12-15 minutes, or until light brown around the edges and soft in the middle. Do not overbake. Transfer to rack to cool.

MAKES ABOUT 4 DOZEN (2-1/2-INCH) COOKIES.

J.B. WILSON'S RESTAURANT & BAR

GONE BUT NOT FORGOTTEN

CHOCOLATE BREAD PUDDING

Ingredients
1 loaf Texas toast
3/4 qt. 40% cream
1 cup milk
1 lb. chocolate chips
1/2 cup sugar
1 tsp. vanilla
4 eggs
1 tsp. cinnamon
1 tsp. nutmeg
1/2 tsp. cloves

Cut bread into small cubes. Place cream, milk and chocolate into a saucepot and heat until chocolate melts and mixture is hot. Mix sugar, vanilla, eggs, and spices in a small mixer with whisk until thick.

In a large bowl, put the sugar and egg mixture in first, then pour in the hot chocolate, stirring constantly. Mix well. Fold in bread and mix well. Let sit for a while, then fold in more bread until bread is soaked all the way through with the chocolate.

Put in a 4-inch hotel pan, cover it with foil and double boil for 30 minutes. Uncover and cook for 15 more minutes.

JOHN CARNEY'S ZABAGLIONE

Ingredients
7 large egg yolks
3/4 cup sweet Marsala wine
1/2 cup sugar
2 tsp. imitation vanilla
2 cups fresh seasonal fruit

PREPARATION

Whip Marsala and sugar over double boiler until sugar is dissolved. Set aside. Whip egg yolks until fluffy. Continue whipping over double boil. Add Marsala and sugar solution slowly to yolks. Continue to whip over double boil until thick and creamy. (Make sure to whip sides of bowl while whipping.) Take off heat and add vanilla. Pour into desired dish. Fold in fresh fruit.

MISSOURI APPLE CRÊPES WITH LEMON-HONEY SAUCE

Crêpe Batter Ingredients
8-12 (10-inch) crêpes
1 cup all purpose flour
1/4 tsp. salt
1 Tbs. sugar
2 large eggs, lightly beaten
1 Tbs. melted butter
2 cups milk
room-temperature butter for greasing pans

PREPARATION

Place the flour, salt and sugar in a bowl and gently stir in the eggs and half the milk until smooth. Continue to stir in the remaining milk and then the melted butter. Let stand at room temperature for 20-30 minutes to rest.

To cook the crêpes, heat your non-stick, 10-inch sauté pan over a medium-high heat and lightly brush or wipe the pan with a little of the room-temperature butter. Ladle 1 ounce of the batter into the center of the pan; immediately tilt and rotate the pan so the batter evenly coats the entire pan. (Remember to gently stir the batter each time you ladle some out.) Let the crepe set up in the pan until the up side looks cooked. Gently turn over the crepe and cook just another one minute on this side.

Slide onto a piece of parchment paper. Repeat this procedure until all the crêpes are cooked. Once cooled, stack the crêpes layered on the paper and cover loosely with a cloth or plastic wrap until ready to serve.

Crepe Filling Ingredients
3 large tart, crisp farm stand apples, peeled, cored and diced
1 tsp. lemon juice
2 Tbs. butter
2 Tbs. sugar
1 Tbs. pure vanilla extract
1/4 cup fresh apple cider

In a non-stick sauté pan, heat the butter until it begins to foam. Add the diced apples and sugar and continue to cook until the apples are lightly browned, stirring the apples from time to time. Add the vanilla and apple cider and continue to cook another minute or two. Set aside in a warm place.

Pick out your best eight crêpes and fill each with 2 Tbs. of the apple mixture, folding over the sides and rolling them into a log (as you would for an egg roll or burrito). When all the crêpes are filled, arrange two on each plate and spoon the honey sauce over the crêpes. Serve with whipped cream.

(Continued)

zest of 1 lemon
juice of 2 lemons
1/4 cup honey (wildflower honey is recommended)
3 Tbs. sweet butter
1 oz. dark rum

In a sauté pan, heat the lemon juice, lemon zest and honey until it begins to bubble. Stir in the butter a tablespoon at a time until incorporated. Add the rum to the pan (NOT OVER THE FLAME!) Move the pan onto the flame and tilt so the pan ignites. Stir until the flames subside.

SERVES 4

LLYWELYN'S PUB

4747 McPherson Ave. 314-361-3003

FUDGE SAUCE

Ingredients
1 cup heavy cream
2/3 cup granulated sugar
6 oz. semi-sweet chocolate
4 Tbs. butter
2 oz. brandy
2 tsp. vanilla extract

PREPARATION

Heat the cream, sugar, chocolate, and butter in small heavy saucepan over low heat, stirring gently until the chocolate melts and the mixture bubbles.

Whisk vigorously until the mixture is smooth and well blended. Heat to boiling and reduce heat to low. Boil gently, stirring frequently, about 5 minutes, using a whisk. Remove from heat and cool slightly. Stir in brandy and vanilla.

Note – this sauce is runny when hot and gets very thick when chilled. Serve either warm or cold. It's great both ways.

Ideas: Put together individual servings of frozen banana slices covered with the fudge sauce. Spoon some cold or hot fudge sauce into a bowl and let your guests dip fresh fruit into it (strawberries, blueberries, banana slices, cherries, grapes, mandarin orange slices, etc.)

Try banana splits (let your guests assemble their own!)
Scoops of ice cream (or yogurt)
Pecans (sauté them in butter)
Strawberries, blueberries, pineapple
Fudge Sauce
Whipped cream
Maraschino cherries
And, of course, wonderful fresh bananas

Store your fudge sauce in the refrigerator. It will stay good for weeks, but it is so good that you may not get a chance to test its longevity.

MAKES 1-1/2 CUPS

LLYWELYN'S PUB

4747 McPherson Ave. 314-361-3003

PRALINE COOKIES

Ingredients
1 stick (4 oz.) salted butter
1/2 cup brown sugar, tightly packed
graham crackers (enough to fill a 9-by-12-inch jelly roll pan)*
10 oz. pecans, chopped
6 oz. semi-sweet or milk chocolate chips

PREPARATION

Preheat oven to 350 degrees. Melt sugar and butter together, being careful not to brown.
Break graham crackers into small rectangles and place them in the pan just as close together as you can get them (we are talking snug here).

Pour the sugar-butter mixture over the crackers and spread evenly. Sprinkle pecans and chocolate chips all over the top. Bake in center of oven for 10 minutes, or until the whole pan comes to a full bubble (when bubbles form in the very center it is cooked).

Remove from oven and let sit for one minute. Separate pieces with a spatula and place them on waxed paper to cool.

The sides of the pan should be a minimum of 1/2-inch high.

GALAKTOBOURIKO (CUSTARD PUDDING)

Ingredients
1/2 lb. pastry sheets (Apollo)
4 eggs
4 cups milk
1/2 cup sugar
1/2 cup "quick" Cream of Wheat (not instant)
2 tsp. vanilla extract
1/2 lb. salted butter
1/2 lb. unsalted butter (melted) for phyllo

Simple Syrup
1-1/2 cups sugar
3/4 cup water
1/2 tsp. vanilla extract
1/2 lemon, sliced

PREPARATION

To make simple syrup, combine all four ingredients in the same saucepan and slowly boil for 8 to 10 minutes. Meanwhile, scald the milk with salted butter. After it boils, add sugar and Cream of Wheat, stirring constantly or you will have lumps. Don't stop until the mixture has thickened (about 10 minutes); put aside to cool slightly.

Butter your 13 x 9-inch pan and line the pan with a pastry sheet. Using melted, unsalted butter (sweetened), brush the sheet. Repeat this step until you have used 8 pastry sheets.

Go back to the Cream of Wheat mixture. Beat eggs and vanilla extract and gradually add to the Cream of Wheat mixture. Refrigerate to cool. Gently pour the cooled Cream of Wheat mixture over pastry sheets, and cover the filling with 12 more pastry sheets. (Each time you add a pastry sheet, you must use your melted unsalted butter in between each layer.)

Fold the pastry sheets tightly on the edges to seal. Refrigerate for 15 minutes, then cut top layer of the pastry sheets before baking. Bake at 350 degrees for about 1 hour (or until you can put a toothpick in and pull it out clean).

During this entire process the simple syrup must be slightly cooled. When the Galaktobouriko is out of the oven, pour the syrup over the hot custard (if syrup is hot when added, it will make the custard mushy). Let it sit for 45 minutes. Cut into squares and serve.

BITTERSWEET CHOCOLATE CAKE

Ingredients
14 oz. butter
10 oz. confectioners sugar
6-1/2 oz. whole eggs
10-1/2 oz. egg yolks
16-1/2 oz. bittersweet chocolate, melted
14 oz. egg whites
4 oz. sugar
5 oz. bread flour, sifted
7 oz. ground, toasted pistachios
7 oz. ground, toasted almonds
1 lb. apricot jam
3 lb. Chocolate ganache (see recipe)

PREPARATION

Using paddle cream butter and confectioners sugar until smooth. Add eggs and yolks until fully incorporated. (Remember to scrape sides of bowl.) Add melted chocolate to egg mixture. Combine egg whites with sugar and whip to medium peaks. Fold meringue into chocolate mixture and add flour and nuts.

Grease and flour 2 (10-inch) cake pans. Divide batter into pans and bake at 350 degrees for 45 - 50 minutes until center springs back. Let cakes cool, then split in half and spread apricot jam on one layer. Put cake back together and ice with ganache.

Chocolate ganache
3/4 lb. bittersweet chocolate
3/4 lb. semi sweet chocolate
1 lb. heavy cream
2 oz. corn syrup

Melt chocolate in double broiler. Heat corn syrup and cream to boil and add to chocolate. Fully incorporate until smooth.

NEW ORLEANS BY-YOU
CRAB SHACK RESTAURANT

GONE BUT NOT FORGOTTEN

PRALINE CANDY

Ingredients
2 cups sugar
1 cup brown sugar
1 cup evaporated milk
1 Tsp. corn syrup
1 Tsp. vanilla (or rum) extract
2 cups nuts (pecans, walnuts, coconut, or almonds)

PREPARATION

Combine sugar and evaporated milk in non-stick saucepan. Using a candy thermometer, bring to a rolling boil at 275 degrees. Add corn syrup. Let it cook until medium brown in color (approx. 30 minutes.) Remove from heat and pour into a large bowl or pan. Let cool for 10 minutes. Add nuts and extract and stir. Drop by spoonfuls onto wax paper.

If properly done, should cool and harden within 5-10 minutes.

THE ORIGINAL PIE PANTRY CO.

301 E. Main, Belleville, IL 618-277-4140

APPLE CREAM PIE

Ingredients
5 cups apples, peeled, cored and sliced
1 cup cream
3/4 cup sugar
4 Tbs. flour
1/4 tsp. salt
3/4 tsp. cinnamon
1 Tbs. sugar

PREPARATION

Place the apples in uncooked pie shell. Mix and pour cream, sugar, flour, salt and 1/2 tsp. cinnamon over apples. Sprinkle sugar and 1/4 tsp. cinnamon mixed over the top.

Bake at 400 degrees for 50-60 minutes.

PORKY'S BACKYARD BARBEQUE

GONE BUT NOT FORGOTTEN

PEACH COBBLER

Ingredients
1 egg
1 cup sugar
3 Tbs. melted butter
1/3 cup milk
1 lemon zest, grated
1 cup all purpose flour
2 tsp. baking powder
1/2 tsp. salt
8 fresh peaches, peeled and sliced
1 Tbs. fresh lemon juice
1 tsp. ground cinnamon
whipped cream or ice cream

Beat together egg, 1/4 cup sugar, butter, milk, and lemon zest. Sift flour, baking powder, and salt into egg mixture and beat thoroughly. Fill half a greased 9 x 12-inch baking dish with peaches and sprinkle with lemon juice. Combine remaining sugar with cinnamon and sprinkle over peaches. Cover with batter and bake at 375 degrees for 30 minutes.

Serve hot or cold, with whipped cream or ice cream.

SQWIRES

1415 S. 18th St. 314-865-3522 www.sqwires.com

BREAD PUDDING

Ingredients
6 egg yolks
6 whole eggs
2 qt. 40% whipping cream
2 vanilla beans, split lengthwise
3 cups sugar
1.5 oz. Kahlua
1.5 oz. Baileys
1.5 oz. Godiva White Chocolate Liquer
2 lbs. brioche bread
cinnamon
white chocolate couverture or chips

PREPARATION

Cream yolks, whole eggs, sugar and alcohol in a bowl. Heat cream and vanilla beans.
Cut brioche into 1-inch squares and put in separate bowl. Bring cream to simmer and take off heat.
Slowly add cream mixture to egg mixture, stirring constantly to avoid cooking eggs. Scrape vanilla
beans and incorporate seeds into mixture.

Pour cream and egg mixture over brioche. Dust with cinnamon and add white chocolate couverture or
chips to mix. Pour into baking pan; bake at 350 degrees for 25 minutes, covered. Uncover and bake
for 15 minutes, until pudding is set and lightly browned.

SERVES 12

TONY'S

410 Market St. 314-231-7007

CRÈME BRÛLÉ

Ingredients
1 pint half and half
4 oz. sugar
1 Tbs. vanilla
2 whole eggs
2 egg yolks
brown sugar

PREPARATION

Bring half and half to a boil with sugar and vanilla. Lightly whip eggs and the 2 yolks. Add the hot half and half mixture to the eggs very slowly. Ladle mixture into shallow custard dishes and bake 40 to 50 minutes at 250 degrees. Cool.

Place a very thin layer of brown sugar on top of custard. Place under broiler until melted and lightly brown. (Watch carefully, as this burns easily.)

TRUFFLES

9202 Clayton Rd. 314-567-9100 www.trufflesinladue.com

CHOCOLATE PUDDING CAKE

Ingredients
16-1/2 oz. bittersweet chocolate
9 egg yolks
9 whole eggs
1 lb. butter
1 cup sugar
1 cup flour

PREPARATION

Whip sugar, yolks, and eggs together. Melt chocolate and butter together and add to sugar and eggs. Add flour slowly to mix. Pour into greased ramekins. Bake in 350-degree oven for 10 to 12 minutes.

GLOSSARY OF COOKING TERMS

AL DENTE- Italian for "to the tooth" used to describe cooked foods, usually pasta and vegetables that are prepared firm to the bite

ARBORIO RICE- Italian grown, high starch, short grain rice used for risotto

ARROWROOT- derived from roots of tropical plants; similar in texture, appearance and thickening power to cornstarch; does not break down as quickly as cornstarch and produces a clearer finished product; more expensive than cornstarch

BLANCHED- very briefly and partially cooking a food in boiling water or hot fat

CARAMELIZE- to heat sugar until it liquefies and becomes a clear syrup ranging in color from golden to dark brown (from 320 to 350 F on a candy thermometer)

CARDAMON- highly aromatic spice; flavor is lemony with notes of camphor and is quite strong and used in both sweet and savory dishes; second most expensive spice in the world

CHAR SIU MARINADE- Chinese marinade for meat (available in jars at Asian markets)

CHIFFONADE CUT- thin strips or shreds of green leafy herbs or vegetables

CLARIFIED BUTTER- a.k.a. drawn butter; unsalted butter slowly melted then water and milk solids removed

COVERTURE CHOCOLATE- high quality chocolate containing at least 32% cocoa butter

BASMATI RICE- rice grown in the Himalayan foothills and preferred in Indian cuisine; highly aromatic with sweet, delicate flavor and creamy yellow color

DEGLAZE- to swirl or stir a liquid (usually wine or stock) in a sauté pan to dissolve cooked food particles remaining on the bottom; the resulting mixture often becomes the base for a sauce

DREDGE- to lightly coat food to be fried with flour, cornstarch, or bread crumbs

FARFALLE NOODLES- bow or butterfly shape pasta

FILÉ POWDER - a seasoning and thickening agent made from dried, ground sassafras leaves

FONTINA CHEESE- Italian semi-firm yet creamy cow's milk with 45% milk fat; mild, nutty

GALAGAL- rhizome with a hot, ginger peppery flavor; used as a seasoning; substitute for ginger

HOISIN SAUCE- thick, sweet, spicy reddish brown sauce used in Chinese cooking; mixture of soybeans, garlic, chile peppers and various spices

JULIENNE- to cut food into stick-shaped pieces 1/8 x 1/8 x 2 inch

GLOSSARY (CONTINUED)

MALAGUETA PEPPER- Brazilian chile pepper

MASCARPONE- Italian buttery-rich cheese made from cow's milk; soft and delicate texture

MATZO MEAL- ground matzo (thin, brittle, unleavened bread)

MIRIN- a.k.a. rice wine; low alcohol, sweet golden wine made from glutinous rice

MOLE PASTE- rich dark reddish brown sauce usually cooked with chicken; generally a smooth, cooked blend of onion, garlic, several varieties of chiles, ground seeds, and a small amount of Mexican chocolate

PALM OIL- reddish oil extracted from pulp of the fruit of the African palm; high in saturated fat, Dende oil is another name for palm oil

PANKO BREAD CRUMBS- Japanese bread crumbs; coarser than American, creating a crunchy crust

PARBOIL- partially cooking a food in boiling or simmering liquid; similar to blanching but cooking time is longer

PEI MUSSELS - Prince Edward Island in Canada is renowned for its high quality mussels

PENETTE- tubular shape pasta

PHAD THAI NOODLES- flat rice noodles

ROUX- cooked mixture of equal parts flour and fat, by weight, used as a thickener for sauces

SCALLOP - a thin, boneless round or oval shaped slice of meat or fish that is usually lightly breaded and quickly sautéed

SEMOLINA- used to make commercially prepared dry pasta products; flour ground from hard drum wheat; has rich cram color and produces very smooth durable dough

SLURRY- a mixture or raw starch and cold liquid used for thickening

SOBA NOODLES- Japanese noodles made from buckwheat and wheat flour

SWEAT- to cook a food (typically vegetables) in a small amount of fat usually covered, over low heat, without browning until the food softens and releases moisture

TAMARIND PASTE- made from the sour-sweet pulp of a fruit that grows on a shade tree in India- when dried it becomes extremely sour; used to flavor curried dishes and chutneys

TASSO- cured pork or beef richly seasoned with Cajun spices like red pepper, garlic, and file powder, as well as other herbs and spices

WATER BATH- container of hot water used to gently cook food or keep food hot

INDEX OF RESTAURANTS

INDEX

INDEX